BURNED IN

Fueling the Fire to Teach

D0111780

BURNED IN

IN

Fueling the Fire to Teach

EDITED BY

Audrey A. Friedman

Luke Reynolds

TEACHERS
COLLEGE
PRESS

Teachers College, Columbia University
New York and London

Published by Teachers College Press, 1234 Amsterdam Avenue, New York, NY 10027

Library of Congress Cataloging-in-Publication Data

Burned in : fueling the fire to teach / edited by Audrey A. Friedman, Luke Reynolds.
    p. cm.
Includes bibliographical references and index.
    ISBN 978-0-8077-5196-1 (pbk.)—ISBN 978-0-8077-5197-8 (hardcover) 1. Teacher morale. 2. Teaching. I. Friedman, Audrey A. II. Reynolds, Luke, 1980–
LB2840.B87 2011
371.102—dc22

2010048815

ISBN 978-0-8077-5196-1 (paper)
ISBN 978-0-8077-5197-8 (hardcover)

Printed on acid-free paper

Manufactured in the United States of America

18 17 16 15 14 13 12 11   8 7 6 5 4 3 2 1

Contents

Introduction

LUKE REYNOLDS

THE MOON WAS FULL AND BRIGHT the night I told my fiancée, Jennifer, that I was going to quit my job as a public high school teacher. It was the end of my first year of teaching 11th-grade, 12th-grade, and journalism classes, and I was completely burned out. Every day I would arrive home to my tiny, above-the-garage apartment and I would sit at my desk, hang my head in my hands, and think: *How can anybody do this job well?*

In my solitude after a full day of teaching, there at my desk, I would review the facts, fears, and foibles of my heart:

- My students don't respect me.
- I am clueless in the classroom.
- My armpits get so sweaty that my shirts soak through, making my students and evaluators think I must have a vendetta against deodorant.
- My voice feels so weak.
- I need more coffee.
- Does every teacher have a bowl of cereal for dinner every night?
- Does every teacher bring home five stacks of 20 five-page essays and pray that God will somehow grade them all by divine appointment?
- I wish I knew more.
- I wish I slept more.
- But I do know something: I love students, I love English, I love the feel of a classroom under my feet, surrounding me.

And yet, I could not find a way to connect my love of students and my passion for my subject to a path forward in my journey. Simply put, I felt as though my fears and inadequacies were far too crushing for me ever to become the kind of teacher I dreamed of being throughout most of my life.

So as my bride-to-be and I sat on my little porch, watching the moon rise, my heart sank. I recall saying, "I just don't think I can do it another year. I don't have what it takes." Jennifer's response saved my life as a teacher: "Just give it one more year. Take the summer to reflect and think, and then go back at it with everything you've got."

Following Jennifer's suggestion, I began a love affair with a profession that still gets me nervous and exhausted—sure—but one in which I feel alive as I contribute to the lives of kids and to the life of our world. Teaching, in essence, became for me a way of living out Robert Frost's poignant definition of poetry: "Words that become deeds."

As I continued my teaching journey, I found that my confidence grew, my connections with students became more and more authentic, my love of the material grew more passionate as I shared it with my kids, and my desire to stand before and beside a group of students who look longingly at the future was unquenchable. But I was amazed at how many *new* teachers would confess to all the same fears and foibles that I had experienced in my first year.

More than once, I was pulled aside by a new teacher who confessed to me, "I think I'm going to quit." And more than once, I tried to say what Jennifer once said to me: *Don't give up yet. Grow. Learn. Fight. Your confidence will increase. Your fears will subside with time and experience.* Wasn't there something that could be done to assuage the crippling state of being a new teacher?

In Ingersoll and Smith's (2004) staggering work on teacher retention, they find that within the first three years of their careers, 50% of all teachers in public schools will quit. We can attribute this massive exit rate to many factors: We can say it's simply because teaching really wasn't for them anyway; we can say that it was because they just couldn't cut it; we can say it was because they wore rose-colored glasses all through their teacher preparation programs. While there may be truth in each of these possibilities—and many others we might conjure up—such prospects do not overshadow the enormity of the crisis. *Half of all people who begin their careers thinking they will love being a teacher decide that they just can't do it.*

Half.

Consider the outcry in our nation if half of all baseball players quit the sport after their first season. Or if half of all elected officials quit their offices after the first year on the job. Or if half of all lawyers quit their jobs after their first year working out of law school. In many other professions we would start to wonder why. And yet, with teaching, we have come to accept that this is the way things are.

Burned In: Fueling the Fire to Teach was conceived and crafted to take up that fight against despair. The essays and reflections in this book all respond, in different ways, to the tragedy of losing hope, losing energy, losing fire. Some voices sing the beauties of the job and illuminate what is at stake within the classroom; other voices rage against the status quo of a system that continues to prefer high-stakes testing and factory-oriented schools over relationships and genuine growth in community; some essayists openly reveal their own journeys and the ways in which they fought past fear, bureaucracy, and despair to become inspiring and committed teachers—teachers with fire for their craft and their calling.

In short, this collection of reflections from teachers, researchers, professors, best-selling authors, and activists offers a path ahead into a territory of hope instead of foraging on the common ground of distress. It is our belief as editors and authors that the words within this book will not only speak to you, but that they will also be words that become deeds in your life as a teacher.

REFERENCE

Ingersoll, R., & Smith, T. (2004, March). Do teacher induction and mentoring matter? *NASSP Bulletin, 88*(638), 28–40.

Chapter 1

Teacher Orientation

JIM BURKE

We will become better teachers not by trying to fill the potholes in our souls but by knowing them so well that we can avoid falling into them.

—Parker Palmer, *Let Your Life Speak*

O UR WORK IS NEVER THE SAME. It makes a complex array of ever-shifting demands on us, each of which has the power to cause in us profound feelings of disorientation that can undermine our ability to do our work or experience the deep sense of purpose and pleasure we sought when we began teaching. We enter into the profession guided by a narrative we have lived, one we have waited to tell about ourselves: becoming the teacher who changes others' lives through our love of students and subject, instilling in students the love of a discipline of which we have now become a disciple. We imagine a life steeped in traditions that go back hundreds of years. During our preparation to become teachers we have been in conversation with ourselves, about who we are, why we are here, and what we will do with our lives. We are, at that point, deeply oriented, our existential compass firmly fixed on the northernmost point of our dreams. Then the bell rings. Kids come. Complexity enters. Life happens.

Our job, to paraphrase William Stafford's poem "Vocation," is to help the world (and our students) find out what it is trying to be. If it were easy, anyone could do it. But it is not and thus takes a very real toll on those who devote their lives to teaching, even as it enriches and gratifies these same people. It is not, of course, just the demands of the work that threaten the fire within us, for this work takes place within the larger context of our lives outside of school, a sphere in which people marry and divorce, give birth to and raise children, care for and bury parents, all while tending to the innumerable mundane aspects of our daily lives that require our time, energy, and attention. If these experiences came in a nice orderly fashion, we might handle them well enough; they do not, however, have a schedule, as we learn all too soon. Indeed, too often they tend to come unannounced, suddenly, and often around the time grades are due. Let us not even get started on the list of factors at school that can further cause in us profound disorientation—unusually difficult classes, larger classes, smaller budgets, new department or school leaders eager to make their mark by replacing their predecessor's efforts with their own brilliant reforms.

Within this whirlwind of confusion that disorientation brings, we find ourselves wondering why we ever thought we could be a teacher, how we ever imagined we would have the strength and resiliency needed to endure the myriad challenges we had not known were part of the landscape of that work. We were so busy telling ourselves a story about the difference we would make in the lives of students whose names we didn't yet know that we forgot to consider that it might not be so easy, that deeper and even darker forces lay ahead, some (physical, emotional, mental problems) lurking within us, while others lay hidden in those we worked with or worked so hard to teach. Thus, especially for the newer, younger teachers among us, a few dark days can throw us into existential despair as we wonder who or what we will be if not a teacher, for so painfully disorientating can such moments of failure—to teach well, to cope with the demands of it all—be that we are left only with the seemingly unshakable truth that we are not supposed to be a teacher, for surely a "real" teacher would never have such feelings, have such disasters, fail in so many ways. All of which is, of course, entirely untrue. But there is no way around such feelings, such experiences, only through them into some new orientation where we begin to discover and develop within ourselves the resiliency, wisdom, and courage needed to teach, lighting our way by the knowledge that being a master teacher is not a destination but a journey through a land that changes as we change, as kids change, as society changes, and as each new year begins.

How we reach this farther, elusive shore of "new orientation" is an important and urgent question. And it is here, in the desert of our disorientation, where we often wander most and feel so lost, that teachers are most vulnerable, most at risk of leaving or losing their love for the profession they dreamed of joining. It is here, as Dante writes, that people feel most profoundly that they have fallen off the path and become lost in the forest, an experience of disorientation—both internal and external, emotional and physical, figurative and literal—that they cannot resolve on their own. In *The Inferno* Dante encounters what we all need if we are to get through to the other side of ourselves and this trouble: a guide, someone who has gone before us and can lead us from where we are to where we hope to be, from the teacher we are to the one we aspire to become. It is not, for any of us, a transformation we can make on our own, though that guide need not be with us in person. Instead, our mentor may come in person or online, through books or at school. Only through this guide, this process, can we achieve the state of new orientation we seek, a state that eventually becomes, once inhabited long enough, our orientation. That is until something new comes along to cause within us, our school, or our lives a new sense of disorientation, at which point the whole cycle begins again.

Every discipline, in some real sense, should cause in each student who engages with it in earnest some sense of disorientation; what is education, after all, if not a call to question everything you think you know is true up to that point about a subject? Even the root of the word *education*, the Latin word *educare*, means "to lead out," to draw out from within one what was there all along and, one might infer, use that to guide oneself through whatever obstacles one will face in the future.

PERSONAL PROFESSIONAL DEVELOPMENT:
THE THREE Rs FOR TEACHERS

And yet we are so often alone in our work; where and how do we find such guidance, especially the type and quality we need? We speak often of students' mastery of the three Rs: reading, writing, and 'rithmetic. And many now talk of students learning the "new three Rs": rigor, relevance, and relationships. Who's to disagree with or question any of these? They are all essential, but impossible to achieve when we are drowning in some new phase of disorientation. Instead, we need a set of three Rs for teachers, a more personal set we can learn to live by heart: reflection, rituals, and relationships.

Reflection calls for us to take time to listen—to ourselves, to our mentors—and consider what we need—for ourselves and from our guides—if we are to move ahead and regain our sense of clarity and purpose. Reflection, while personal, need not be silent or done alone. It is as likely to involve reading authors like those you find included in this volume as it is to involve writing. While you can certainly go to the café to write in a journal about what is going on in your life or your classroom, you can also meet friends there, as I so often see people do at the café I frequent, and let them be your mirror as you reflect, through discussion, on your work and life. Such reflective conversations for me often take place while going for a walk to the café near school as a colleague and I talk there about teaching, kids, and life. Nor does the writing need to take place in the privacy of a journal; it can, if one finds the right community, happen online in a community such as the one I created (www.englishcompanion.ning.com) where thousands of English teachers come to help one another solve the problems inherent in the work. It is through such reflection that teachers re-collect and re-create themselves and in the process regain their sense of direction, moving through their disorientation into the greater resiliency of new orientation.

The act of reflection is, of course, a *ritual*; these three Rs by no means exclude one another. In fact, they might be best represented as a three-part Venn diagram to visually emphasize their integration, their interdependence. Ritual can, as I have already mentioned, mean going to a place (café, meditation center, forest) and engaging in an activity (writing, meditation, walk). It can also mean engaging in activities that reinforce our commitment to our own growth and well-being: exercise, classes, church, or reading; it is during such rituals, or the practice of such rituals, that our guides can make the biggest difference, offering us suggestions about what to read or what to do, how to think, what to learn.

Finally, it is through our *relationships* with these guides and other critical friends that we achieve the growth we need to continue on. Some of these relationships are based on what they tell us to do or read. I have enjoyed a long string of colleagues, both men and women, always older, to whom I have turned for guidance and wisdom about what to read—or even just the continuing affirmation that I must read, that nothing can make more of a difference for me in terms of professional and intellectual growth. But we need more from these relationships than book recommendations! We need community, the intimacy of conversation. For years I have gone to dinner a few times a year with two women from school— one a special education teacher, the other an ESL teacher; we go to the same restaurant (a lovely little bistro in San Francisco) where we always get the same seat (which we call our "tree house," as it is nestled away in a corner by a window). We enjoy a good meal, have a nice bottle of red wine, and then walk down to the same French café for espresso afterward to continue our talk and get some air. This ritual has sustained each of us through periods of personal and professional disorientation. And, as I've already mentioned, other kinds of relationships can now exist, offering a deep sense of companionship and intimacy, through online communities, Skype, and even Twitter (despite the 140-character limit).

LIVING THE CYCLE

Now that I've been teaching for 20 years, one would think I have graduated from the cycle, that I moved through it, learned the lessons, and achieved some Nirvana-like release from the cycle, settling into the comfortable orientation of mastery. I wish it were so, but it is not. This year's freshmen class is unlike any before it; little of what I have taught before is working, thus forcing me to assess and create new ways to meet their needs. Our school has just been declared a Program Improvement school, a declaration that mandates that we begin to change everything we do to meet new federal requirements no one will clearly explain to us. A new principal this year brings new ways, new ideas, some of which he shares with us, others of which he does not, and none of which show any substantial wisdom, but then what can one expect from an administrator who makes up the agenda (on a sticky note in his hand) as he stands up in front of us trying to finish the meeting as soon as possible?

I don't mean to sound a cynical note; rather, I aim only to illustrate how volatile our work can be within the class and the larger community of the school. If, despite the swirl of chaos we call our work, we are to be strong and effective, to love and to last in our work, to live to tell the story we came in as young teachers wanting to tell about ourselves, we must use the three Rs I've proposed above to help us throughout the cycle. Then, instead of getting off the cycle of our own learning and life, it will be our turn to do for others what so many have done for us, especially in those early years: guide them through the dark days of their disorientation so that they, like Dante emerging from the underworld, will see the stars and know again the beauty of the world in which they have learned to work—and live.

Chapter 2

Burn On, Teacher!
(But Where's That Lighter?)

Michael Dunn

YOU NEVER FORGET YOUR FIRST CLASS. Fresh out of college, as idealistic as they come, I was beginning a year volunteering at an all-boys Catholic high school in the Bronx, teaching religion and English to classes with 35 sophomore boys in each. It was early September 1990, and the hair was in the style of those square-cut Afros of the time. Their names and faces are indeed "burned in": Jamie from Puerto Rico, Ed from Bulgaria, Declan from Ireland, LeShawn from Jamaica, Carlos from the Dominican Republic. I still see them, wearing blue jackets and thin ties, waiting to find out if the newbie had the faintest clue what he was doing. They soon found out.

I began with an overhead transparency of my favorite prayer—the Prayer of St. Francis—asking them to read it along with me: "Lord, make me an instrument of your peace. . . . Where there is darkness, let me sow light . . ." A few read, many mumbled, and some seemed to be breathing somewhat heavier than the situation should warrant. As I went on with my lesson, heads began dropping onto bent elbows. After a few minutes I noticed Carlos in the front row making some sort of tally on his desk. When I asked him about it, he said that's how many times I had said "Um" so far (42), and the period wasn't even half gone.

I hadn't a clue what I was doing, nor an ounce of preparation, but through sheer persistence and a sense of humor, I survived. Now, 20 years on, beginning my 18th year teaching English at a suburban high school in Connecticut, my 3rd year leading the English department, I know who I am: I'm an educator; it's burned in, to be sure, branded on my being. I can't hear an NPR story on my way to work without thinking of a connection to class. Saturday while coaching Michael's soccer game, I found myself teaching players on the opposing team how to keep both feet on the ground for a throw-in. Yesterday I handed the screwdriver to Sean when he asked me to fix the chain guard on his bike. I remember pointing to every word each time I read *Brown Bear, Brown Bear, What Do You See?* to Mary when she was a few weeks old. And you should hear how many metaphors I was able to hide behind (electrical outlets, chili powder, etc.) when Fiona asked me last summer, "Dad, what's sex?"

But who are *you*? As I teach my students in room 911 (yes, that's really my room number), a writer should keep his audience in mind. But who would pick up a book with a title like *Burned In*? New teachers often have fuel and fire enough, and many educators I know, new or veteran, are too busy to read much for pleasure. Maybe you're an aspiring student teacher questioning whether this is the profession for you. Or maybe you're an administrator researching possible inspiration to rekindle teachers you supervise, some of whom may be more burned *out* than *in*. Whoever you are, I know who *I* am. But, at this midpoint of my career, I admit to having felt at times a bit more like picking up such a book than putting something in it. So, no offense to you, aspiring newbie or inspiring leader, I'm compelled to write this for those of my colleagues whose knees are dirty from blowing ashes off the embers.

Don't get me wrong—I love teaching. There's really nothing like it: each day we get to grow human beings and get paid to do it. Encouraging students as they struggle to make meaning of a complex text, helping them dig under the surface of their first few drafts to uncover what really wants to be written, exhorting them to consider opposing arguments when trying to persuade, collaborating with colleagues to craft lesson plans and create engaging student tasks, all of this is satisfying work, and there's no buzz quite like the buzz of an effective lesson. On a larger scale, I'd go so far as to argue that there's no job as important, as noble and time-honored, as essential not only for our species to survive but to thrive. Teachers can count among our lucky many no less than the likes of the Buddha, Confucius, Socrates, Jesus, and Annie Sullivan—miracle workers all. As other contributors to this volume may attest, little has been tried or created and few lives have been changed without, in some form or another, the touch of a teacher. At the bottom of it all is that we humans are most alive, most in tune with the music of the spheres, when we are learning. And educating, among the many noble and time-honored professions of the Earth, holds the greatest potential to plant our feet firmly along this quest.

All this is true, but such truth doesn't bring home much bacon, and according to a poll in the cover story of a recent *Time,* three out of four Americans believe "teaching is among the most underappreciated professions in the U.S." and that "many of the smartest people in society don't go into teaching because being a teacher doesn't pay enough" ("Americans' views on teacher tenure," 2010). The inherent pun in the title to this book you're holding wouldn't work without the implied reality of its flame-dousing shadow side, whispering that there's something in the nature of the job that can lead its practitioners to burn *out* rather than *in.*

Maybe it's because of how out of shape I got this past year under the onslaught of papers to grade, grades to enter, lessons to plan, essential questions to revise, standards to assess, assessments to craft, rubrics to align, student work to examine, data to analyze, interventions to implement, reports to write, observations to write up, team meetings and committee meetings and department meetings and department leader meetings and curriculum meetings to plan, documents to create and digest, articles to read, e-mails to reply to, parents to contact, students to counsel, letters of recommendation to write, battles to fight, conflicts to resolve, and fires to put out that arise in the daily work of leading and managing human beings amidst increasingly limited resources and often competing needs. Maybe it's easy to get lost in a jungle of jargon, buried under an avalanche of acronyms (a partial list includes CAPT, CMT, DRP, AP, SAT, PSAT, UbD, and RTI, each generating its own spreadsheet) that can feel more corporate or bureaucratic than may appeal to the sensibilities of people who chose not to go into corporate bureaucracy. Maybe the ground is shifting so fast under our feet, and there's more pressure than ever and from more directions. Maybe the job simply can't be done without reserves of positive energy, and everyone seems to have more to complain about these days.

"Suck it up! Some of us work for a living!" (Yes, aspiring newbie, if you're still with me, get ready to hear this gem, even at family parties.) I'm never one to suggest there aren't plenty of other complex or underappreciated jobs out there, which may have as many acronyms to decipher and could just as easily lead to burnout. Perhaps they should have their own books. And yes, there are pauses built into the current cycles of the school year that do afford some chance of renewal, although "off" ain't what it used to be when our To Do list is cluttered into those spaces. The number of nights I stay at school until eleven just to catch up has increased rather than decreased over the past few years, just when I thought things would get easier with time. Finally, as I seek a wider classroom and as we plan for college, I've begun saying goodbye to room 911 to go full-time into leadership. I know I'll miss my classroom terribly, but it's precisely the teacher in me that feels compelled to share what I've learned about teaching with other teachers. I also know the "dark side" jokes often stem from competing attitudes about how best to quantify quality, and I've known many educational leaders as "burned in" as I am.

Walking in some waves with Kathleen and the kids did blow ashes off my embers, but how can we maintain our fire in the midst of all the drizzle? Two simple lessons come to mind, one yin, the other yang. The yin is the very first advice I got before heading to the Bronx, given to me in no uncertain terms by my Uncle Al, the tough, strong-armed principal of a Long Island high school who had also equipped me with my first catcher's mitt 10 years earlier. When I asked Uncle Al for any words of wisdom, I expected something I could put on a poster or find on a Hallmark card. Instead he gazed piercingly at me and simply said, with conviction, *Illegitimus non tatem carborundum!*"—and told me to look it up. When I did, I discovered the Latin might be more accurately rendered *"Illegitimi non carborundum,"* and means "Don't let the bastards grind you down." Not the sunniest sentiment, to be sure, but, not realizing it at the time, this would somehow come to be the single piece of advice I've passed along more than anything else. From counseling colleagues how to survive the prickly parent or pile of papers, or how to hone meaning from the jungle of jargon, Uncle Al's advice has grown more relevant with time.

The rub about educating is that it can, if you're not careful, grind the best of us down, burn anyone out, no matter how strong the steel or bright the flames at the outset. There are always more problems to solve, more demands on teachers and leaders and schools than ever before. Even this far along in my career I need to remind myself that it's often a simple matter of pacing—keep your head about you, do the best you can, keep the "bastards" at bay, and be mindful of what fuels you.

This is a start, but merely maintaining the fire is a pretty low standard. What *is* it that fuels us? This brings me to my second epiphany, the brighter and warmer yang to Uncle Al's rather grim yin—the recognition of the most important guiding star, right in front of my nose the whole time, like the scarlet-sequined gleam from Dorothy's slippers: It's not about *us*, it's about *them*. Paraphrasing Clinton's 1992 campaign, "It's the Students, Stupid!" It's the realization that just about nothing I've said about raining ash onto the flames has to do with the students themselves, that much of it simply obscures the thing that got us all attracted to the flames in the first place, that the very source of the light and heat in the fragile embers of teaching is the light and heat it stokes in our learners. It's not the act of teaching—the coaching, explaining, advising, suggesting, modeling, counseling—because what human being can be fully alive without doing these things once in a while? It's when we forget that it's about the fire inside the students, equipping them to figure things out for themselves, challenge and defend their points of view, pursue their passions, and find ways to use the stuff of life to find meaningful metaphors for the turbulence of growing up in this frenetic world.

Very simply, I keep educating because they keep making new people, and I don't just mean this in the job-security sense. Each fall there's a whole new crop of human beings to grow, who never knew they could write a sonnet, or how effectively they are "played" each day by advertisers, or how blessed they are to be able to question their government, or how passionate Emily Dickinson really was, or how to sift through an Internet full of crap to find a source worth quoting. I've taught certain texts until I can quote a good bit of them by heart, but I haven't seen *these* kids make their own discoveries about them. In the end the only thing that really lights the fire is what lights up the torch Lady Liberty holds high above us, the light of freedom itself. Our goal is the learning, not the teaching, and our ultimate prize is when we see our students standing confident and independent and free, doing it all without any more help from us. Our job is to equip them and build their capacity, but in the end they're the ones who have to score the goal, fix the bike, and figure out truth and beauty and meaning all by themselves.

Almost everything we experienced when we were students seems to be changing. No longer is it about passing on answers to questions—it's about teaching them how to ask questions and stoking the ones they already have. No longer is it about reading texts because they are classic, it's about reading them to figure out if they still earn that distinction, and leading learners to make and reflect on their own choices. As the ground shifts, we have to keep our eyes on the prize. It's only when students are discovering, inquiring, getting messy, composing, revising, performing, stretching beyond their previous notions of the possible, and getting fired up, that we ignite again our own blaze.

As I ponder my path outside of room 911, knowing all of this has been "burned in," I also know that many of the things that can seem like jargonized acronyms are often tools to build this vision, and that what applies to good teaching also applies to good leading. From the "gradual release" of workshop classrooms to the focus on authentic performance assessments like capstone projects, a movement is well under way to articulate new goals and standards responsive to the demands of learning and living in these constantly changing times; and much of current research and "best practice" reflects this shift in the direction of real student inquiry. The first task of leadership is to provide the supports teachers need to engage collaboratively in this inquiry in sustained and meaningful ways; and with new technologies emerging every day and new ways to assess student performance, to use data wisely as the tool that it is to help us help our students grow ever more accomplished and confident in their skills and understandings. Many districts, such as mine, take seriously their efforts to incarnate our beliefs that *all* students can and will expand their possibilities, and provide time for teachers to collaborate to write and revise curriculum, share student work, and learn with one another to create solutions to problems.

Before my mom left home each morning to nurse her patients at the hospital where each of us was born, she would joke, "I'm off to save lives and stamp out disease." This year I closed our first department meeting by sharing this, to remind my teachers of our own high calling, each and every ordinary day, "to grow people and stamp out ignorance and fear." If you decided to hang in there, aspiring newbie, I hope I've been crystal clear—this won't be easy, and the world may not value your work, and there will be times when you feel it all grinding you down. But there really is nothing as important. Maintain and stoke your fire, tapping what's always fueled it by creating opportunities for kids to ask their own questions, make and learn from their own mistakes, write what they choose, explore their own passions, and collaborate with each other to find their own ways to create light and warmth in what the TV clicker can suggest is a dark, cold, and angry world. A moment's connection with another human, in the seat next to them or in the text in front of them, or a moment's awareness of a blade of grass surging through a sidewalk crack, can remind us of the million tiny ways we can fulfill our real mission: to spread our light and warmth in order to fuel this fragile fire we call human life on planet Earth.

I'm not one of those educators who always knew I wanted to do this. It wasn't until high school that I began to connect my quest to help make the world a little better with early stirrings to give this gig a try. In college I gathered up as many an inspiring educational experience as I could, fell more deeply in love with truth and beauty and justice, and became ever more committed to my dawning notion that education is our last best hope to save and evolve the species. Filled with fire and hope as I rode the Metro North train from New Haven to the Bronx, I filed Uncle Al's advice away, completely unaware of how soon, or how often, I'd need it.

I loved those kids, have in fact loved all my students, if love can be defined by willing the good for another person, and that's really the point. Though a few certainly gave it a good shot at times, I didn't let them grind me down. What's really burned in is the learning, not the teaching: the memories and experiences, snapshots in the highlight film, I can still see and feel so vividly. I can still see the green leaves turning crimson above the mist that October day I coached my Bronx JV soccer team, fourteen 15-year-olds born in thirteen different countries, in that epic battle they fought so valiantly against that wealthy Westchester school, which we lost on the last penalty kick after three overtimes. I can still see Julio, who, like every one of them, played his heart out, clutching his bleeding knee, tears wetting his jet-black lashes, hobbling back to join the motley crew that had suddenly transformed into a team. Now, beginning anew, I see the snapshots spark high from the crackling fire, lighting my way forward once again:

- Shaking my head in wonder as Jeff, Becky, Tim, and Justin and my six other alternative school students, who had just driven me batty on the bus, listen with respectful admiration to the Iwo Jima survivor on our field trip to the local Marine memorial.
- Silently cheering from the back of the room as super-shy Michelle, who reluctantly enrolled in our AP English language class to pacify her parents, overcomes her fears to stand in front of the class presenting her final project exploring her passion for graffiti art.
- Seeing, through a thousand and one writing conferences, human miracles emerge right in front of me.
- Smiling this morning as her classmates helped Gina apply her rhetorical skills to convince me to let her eat her apple in class.

- . . . and all the rest, as ordinary and miraculous as wood catching a spark, enough to fill up this whole book. I've learned a lot since my first day, but my prayer remains the same: to shed light where there is darkness, and to stoke the flames when the ashes pile up too high. Lord, when I forget, remind me where the fire comes from!

REFERENCE

Americans' views on teacher tenure, merit pay and other education reforms. (2010, September 20). *Time.* http://www.time.com/time/nation/article/0,8599,2016994,00.html#ixzz1ALnFypx4

Chapter 3

Getting Burned

ANDY HARGREAVES

IDON'T TEACH CHILDREN ANY MORE. Not directly, anyway. I teach adults who teach children. I try to keep a little bit of the child alive in all of them, of course. Just as importantly, I try to keep a bit of that child alive in myself—hopeful, passionate, playful, committed, trusting, resilient, and optimistic. In my life as a professor, I'm a writer and a researcher. I'm a consultant, a coach, and a supervisor. But more than anything, first and last, I'll always be a teacher. It's one of the very best things to be.

You might say it's easy to get excited about teaching when you're teaching highly educated adults. And in many ways, you'd be right. Mostly, they don't show up really late; they've usually eaten before they come to class; they don't intimidate their professors; and they don't beat each other up. And it's easy to be inspirational when you only have to teach two or three classes every week instead of four or five or even more every day. Any professor who claims they are burned out, you can argue, is just a whiny princess who can't even abide an infinitesimally small pea.

And yet, for all the advantages of academic life, there are professorial colleagues who do come to manifest that "deadening of the intellect" that Willard Waller harshly claimed afflicted the psyche of schoolteachers in his classic book *The Sociology of Teaching* in 1932. Not many people talk about burnout in academic life. Indeed, the whole idea of academic burnout might strike many other people like emergency room doctors, grief counselors, or troops in combat as just an outrageous oxymoron.

19

Yet the work of the university professor is speeding up just as much as the work of teachers and many other professions. Publish or perish, the race toward tenure, the demands to bring in big research grants, proposal after proposal, committee upon committee, project teams to manage, students who need supervising, others who question their grades, calls for your service by the wider profession either to advise about something here or talk to that group there, classes to prepare, papers to grade, and collegial envy and jealousy running rife throughout the academy—these are the ever-pressing parameters of professorial life. And as professors get older (and some of us are becoming quite old indeed), the body isn't always as resilient as it once used to be, either.

The late Seymour Sarason (a living antithesis of burnout when still writing in his 90s) drew on the work of Cherniss (1980) to describe burnout as "a change in attitude and behavior in response to a demanding, frustrating, unrewarding work experience. "The dictionary defines 'to burn out' as ' to fail, wear out, or become exhausted by making excessive demands on energy, strength or resources'" (Sarason, 1982). Among human service professionals, he says, burnout has become associated with "negative changes in work-related attitudes and behavior in response to job stress." One of the major effects is "loss of concern for the client and a tendency to treat clients in a detached, mechanical fashion." Burnout is not an attritional process of aging, but an emotional process of being overloaded and undervalued.

The people most prone to burnout are not those who are the least committed. You can't burn out if you've never been alight. The ones who burn out are often those who care the greatest, give the most. When you've too many people to see, you can go home feeling you've never seen enough of any of them. When you're deluged by paper, it's hard to be devoted to all your people. When you keep the candle burning at one end for the project deadline, or the conference paper, or the reference you have to write for someone, it's desperately hard to keep it flickeringly brightly at the other end, for every student and colleague, all the next day. And if all this is hard for privileged professors, imagine what it's like when you work in the front line of fire in urban public schools.

Some years ago, I studied how elementary teachers used their time (Hargreaves & Tucker, 1991). What they repeatedly talked about was their feelings of guilt. They experienced what is called *depressive guilt*—not the guilt of having a wrongdoing found out, but the guilt that comes from feeling you are hurting those for whom you care by never being able to care enough. An intense orientation to caring for the young and the vulnerable, combined with classroom conditions that restricted resources and created shortages of time, left some of the most dedicated teachers feeling they were always falling short.

This work on guilt led me to make a systematic attempt to investigate the emotions of teaching more generally—the factors that created positive and negative emotion in teachers' work (Hargreaves, 1998). We interviewed 50 elementary and secondary teachers and began to look at what sociologist Arlie Hochschild (1983) termed the *emotional labor* that is required and performed by those who work in the people professions. Emotional labor, Hochschild said, was the labor involved in having to manage your feelings to meet the expectations of the job—calmness and kindness in a flight attendant, irritability in a debt collector, and caring in a nurse. Even when clients were difficult and working conditions were poor, those in the people professions had to engage in a kind of acting: making themselves feel things they didn't initially feel or suppressing the feelings they did feel.

Teachers we interviewed reported many incidents of exercising emotional labor in their work. Having to be enthusiastic with your class when you felt really tired, needing to remain calm with an irate parent, suppressing an urge to criticize a colleague to his face—this was the emotional life that seemed to accompany the job. Some of this emotional labor, we found, was a labor of love. When the emotional labor helped teachers reach their children, bring lessons alive, reassure parents, and motivate colleagues, it was labor worth expending. This was even more true when work conditions gave teachers the freedom to inspire their students and the time to know them well.

But emotional labor was seen as negative and debilitating when it had to serve other people's imposed purposes and when there was o time to care for people properly. Hochschild found this to be the case when the flight attendants she studied had their work speeded up, their crew numbers reduced, and their tasks increased in order to cut costs and increase airline efficiency. The flight attendants' response was either to work harder and harder until they became exhausted, or to leave the job for something else, or to persuade themselves that passengers had changed and were no longer worth caring for, thus managing their own inability to care by diminishing the deservingness of their passengers.

Public school teachers in run-down urban schools respond in the same way. In the United States and Canada, when standardized educational reforms, prescribed programs, overtested assessment regimes, and cutbacks in resources began to take a grip on schools, my colleagues and I interviewed well over 200 high school teachers about the effects of this new climate on their work (Hargreaves, 2003). Here are some of our findings:

- *There was less creativity.* Teachers described having to "teach to the test instead of being creative"; "feeling forced to leave out interesting exercises"; and being "too busy to try" being creative. In the words of one teacher, "creativity and enthusiasm have become hopelessness and depression, and a lethargic outlook has evolved."
- *There was demoralization, literally loss of purpose.* Teachers had a "feeling of betrayal." They were "tired of being bashed" by the government. One spoke for many colleagues when he said, "I'm a good teacher. I love teaching, and I really enjoy working with teenagers. But right now I am so depressed about the politics surrounding teaching that I sometimes don't know how I will go on!"
- *There was an exodus from the profession.* Those who could leave, did. Because of the negative attitude of the government and deteriorating working conditions, teachers had "firmly decided to leave," would be "leaving the profession as quickly as I can," and "looked forward to retirement." Teachers were becoming "very, very burned out."

The young were becoming disillusioned, not just the old. "There is no joy in teaching," said one, "only a paper trail of grief." Another who "loved to teach" was "seriously considering leaving the profession. I surely wouldn't wish this profession on my children," he said. He "loved working with children, but not with this government."

How can teachers and schools counter these tendencies toward burnout? They can care less, of course, conserving their energy and diminishing the flame. But in the end, it is Sarason, the community psychologist, who holds the key. If teachers are going to be able to keep on giving, he says, they have to experience more getting. You cannot keep drawing on the well without replenishing the sources of supply.

Paradoxically, a lot of what you get in teaching comes back from the very people who are the beneficiaries of your giving—your students. Back from several days of intensive fieldwork, jet-lagged from a transatlantic flight, tired after 10 hours of back-to-back meetings, I don't always feel at my best when I start my evening graduate classes. And with many students coming in after long days at school, a 7 p.m. class in the middle of January is not always the most energizing prospect for them either. But very soon, the discussion gets going, the questions begin, the engagements intensify, souls open up, and eyes light up with them. At the end of a good night, after 5 hours of classes, together we defy the second law of thermodynamics and all leave with more energy than we brought into the room—giving each other energy we never even knew we had stored somewhere deep within us.

In the most cited book on the work of teaching ever, Dan Lortie (1975) described what teachers were getting from their students as the *psychic rewards* of teaching. Unlike lawyers, teachers did not know whether they had won or lost. Nor could teaching tell them whether their students were cured or not. So teachers' rewards became personal, emotional, or "psychic." But here Lortie offered only faint praise. The rewards supposedly rested on exceptional individual cases of child rescue in the present and deferred praise from students who returned far in the future. What Lortie didn't also acknowledge was the sheer joy teachers experience with whole classes as well as individuals, now and not just in the future.

Every teacher knows this. There is intense joy in teaching when children stumble through their first words for the first time, when a student from a poor family who has struggled desperately hard in your class makes the grade to get to college, when a once-bullying child puts his arm around a neighbor whose pet just passed away, and when you successfully try out a new teaching strategy that hasn't quite worked before or get a difficult point across that you used to stumble over previously. Getting positive feedback from your principal, hearing your students praise *you*, seeing their passions get ignited, the lightbulbs going on—these are the moments when teaching gets you burned in, not burned out. Like a tattoo or a brand, this is what gets teaching under the skin and keeps teachers going even when everything outside the classroom conspires to defeat them.

It will always be the case that the most heroic and resilient teachers will be able to cocoon themselves in their classes and take pleasure from these satisfactions, despite all the policies and innovations that are imposed upon them. But if we are to get greater success in many urban schools and classes, it's time to stop racing to the top with more demands, more pressures, more haste, and less speed. Unless teachers get more training before they are thrown into urban classrooms, unless underperforming schools get help from better schools rather than being bullied by superiors above them, unless principals know and care about the teachers they are expected to evaluate, and unless praise is put before blame and help is offered before harassment, then America's much hailed Race to the Top will simply push too many teachers over the edge so they go hurtling to the bottom.

In teaching, there is only one thing worse than burnout and that's a flame that's never been ignited. Demeaning teachers, closing their schools, attacking their unions, standardizing their teaching, saying everything is broken, and testing everything else to death will simply return public education to an emotional Stone Age, where the fire has still to be lit.

REFERENCES

Cherniss, C. (1980). *Professional burnout in human service organizations.* New York: Praeger.

Hargreaves, A. (1998). The emotions of educational change. In A. Hargreaves, A. Lieberman, M. Fullan, & D. Hopkins (Eds.), *The international handbook of educational change* (pp. 558–570). The Netherlands: Kluwer Publications.

Hargreaves, A. (2003). *Teaching in the knowledge society.* New York: Teachers College Press.

Hargreaves, A., & Tucker, E. (1991). Teaching and guilt: Exploring the emotions of teaching. *Teaching and Teacher Education, 7*(5/6), 491–505.

Hochschild, A. (1983). *The managed heart: Commercialization of human feeling.* Berkeley: The University of California Press.

Lortie, D. (1975). *Schoolteacher.* Chicago: University of Chicago Press.

Sarason, S. (1982). *The culture of the school and the problem of change.* Boston: Allyn & Bacon.

Waller, W. (1932). *The sociology of teaching.* New York: Wiley & Sons.

Chapter 4

Subject Love

ROSETTA MARANTZ COHEN

OR THE PAST 25 YEARS I have been investigating the mysteries of veteran teacher commitment, those peculiar traits of
character and intellect that allow certain teachers to remain
deeply engaged and invested in the profession over long periods of
time while others burn out or grow bored and indifferent to the
work. Back in the mid-1980s my doctoral dissertation tracked the
careers of five veteran teachers working in large suburban schools
who were still passionate and enthusiastic about teaching after
spending upwards of 30 years in the field. Later, I looked at urban
teachers who displayed the same traits: a strange and wonderful
resilience to the assaults of bureaucratic idiocy, misbehavior, and
overwork.

But the subject of teacher commitment had been interesting to
me long before I started any graduate work. I grew up in a family
where professional passion was a daily object lesson. My mother, a
French teacher in a regional New Jersey high school, was literally
obsessed with her work. In the 1960s and 1970s she was the only
working mother among all my friends, and though my father's salary alone was certainly adequate to support our family, she would
never have dreamed of quitting. From the moment she began to
work, teaching became the center of her life. Being a French teacher, she used to say, "defined her" and justified her "existence on
earth"; it gave her credibility in a world where women's identities
were often circumscribed by narrow domestic strictures, and it provided a safety net in case of financial disaster (a condition that, as a
child of the Depression, she always vaguely feared). But my moth-

er's devotion to teaching extended beyond the existential and the practical: more than anything, she just loved French; she just loved France. Everything about the language and the country appealed to her. Growing up in a small Brooklyn apartment, the child of Russian immigrants, my mother first got hooked on French in high school, where the language came to represent a new and dazzling world of beautiful clothes, art, intense feeling, and delicious food, a world driven and defined by the kind of high aesthetic that could transport and redeem her. For the rest of her life, including her long career in the classroom, my mother's love of French never wavered. She reveled in teaching it, dancing around her classroom in a cloud of French perfume, dressing in French miniskirts purchased during yearly pilgrimages to Paris, and coaxing stuttered phrases out of two generations of dazzled and adoring students. Years ago, when I interviewed my mother for a research project on veteran teachers, I asked her to cite the one trait that teachers need most to sustain themselves over time. Love of subject, she had said immediately. "More than anything," she said, "you have to love your subject."

Such a response, I found out, was unusual in the literature. When I started investigating the mysteries of happy veterans, I found that accepted theories of teacher retention tended to focus on other traits of character. Indeed, according to research, committed veteran teachers tended to fall into one of two categories: (1) those who love children and who sustained themselves by their continual delight in the charms of the young; and (2) those who saw their work as larger than themselves, as a kind of spiritual calling— a belief that could work handily to bolster resolve in hard times.

But since my own first study in the 1980s, I've yet to find significant research that looked specifically at "love of subject" as an incentive for long-term commitment. This is interesting to me because my own anecdotal experience with veteran teachers over the years has turned up quite a number who fall into this category. Many of our friends are high school teachers who came to the work after failing to finish doctoral dissertations, or because their spouses had found employment in places where their own aspirations to become college professors could not be satisfied.

These people are all lovers of subject—teachers who actively read and study in their fields simply for the pleasure of it. High school teaching allows them time to read and think, without imposing on them the pressures of publication.

Indeed, my own husband, Sam, is a prime example of this particular kind of veteran teacher. An all but dissertation Ph.D. candidate who subordinated his ambitions to those of his wife, Sam is now in his 30th year as a passionate, inspired high school English teacher. When I ask Sam what sustains him, he answers exactly as my mother did: literature sustains him, he says, and gives dignity to an enterprise that is sometimes—to use Sam's words—"demeaning, demoralizing, and depressing." Unlike my mother, who taught in an affluent suburban school, Sam is an urban teacher who daily contends with both the pleasures and difficulties of working with a very diverse population of students. Like many teachers, he likes young people; and like many teachers, he sees his work as important. But like my mother, the overriding incentive to stay in the field is Sam's abiding love of fiction, poetry, and the endless volumes of literary criticism that he reads for fun—the way I read *US magazine* and *Vanity Fair*. For Sam, the two sections of AP English Literature that he teaches each day make it possible for him to continue to teach his "lower-level" classes with energy and enthusiasm. He needs his daily "fix" of literature and a forum for speaking about books in serious and complex ways. Were these courses taken away from him, I'm sure that Sam would burn out fast. "I entered teaching," Sam says, "because I loved literature—I literally worshipped at the altar of the Great Dead—and I was looking for a way to just read and think for a living. Though jobs come and go, colleagues come and go, students get better or worse—that love never wavers."

Recently, I have been doing research on international veteran teachers, English teachers from all over the world, including areas like remote Tipo-Tipo in the Philippines or war-torn Yemen or postcommunist Romania and Poland. The teachers who submit these essays are among the best and most successful practitioners in their respective countries; they have all been awarded Fulbright or State Department grants to study American culture, and they write with passion and fluency about what they do. As part of this project, I have asked these teachers to describe those factors that have allowed them to stay fresh and committed to the field over long periods of time. Predictably, some teachers speak to the pleasures of working with children; others describe the political impact a teacher can make. But a significant number of these teachers speak to the "pleasures of subject" as the sustaining force in their work. Among these international teachers, passion for subject (in this case, English) functions very much in the same way that it does for Sam—as a buffer against bureaucracy, squalid teaching conditions, poor resources, and student indifference. Viktor, for example, a long-time veteran from a remote area of Siberia called Sakha-Yakutia, writes that his love of the English language has redeemed his life from barrenness and depression. Teaching in a small cinderblock school during the dark days of Soviet repression, Viktor says he came to associate the sound of English with all things bright and free. "Children, I was indifferent to," he writes, "and the curriculum was as dead and boring as you can imagine. But I had a record of English Christmas songs, and I played it over and over, and the sound of the language really sustained me. I was drawn to it like it was a magnet." Victor's comments reminded me of my mother's love for French; he describes that inexplicable pull of subject that seems to come from nowhere and that explains, more than anything, his commitment to the field.

Anna, from Poland, reminds me of Sam. Anna speaks in her essay about the changes that have happened to the Polish school system since the fall of the Berlin Wall. Even though teaching under the rigid communist regime inhibited creative freedom, writes Anna, teachers were still deeply respected—even revered. Under the post-Soviet system discipline has deteriorated and fewer students are willing to engage intellectually. "Everyone is out to make a buck," she writes. "There is less interest in literature and the humanities, as everyone wants to become a businessman or a politician." For Anna, the pleasures of teaching have been stripped away by this cultural shift. All that remains is her love of literature. "I teach one class on American literature to advanced students," she writes. "At this point, at my age, that is the only thing that keeps me in the field."

After so many years, it still confounds me that research pays so little heed to "subject passion" as a factor in teacher retention. Such research, after all, would be welcome news to budget-conscious school districts. Passion for subject is a trait that doesn't cost a school anything; there are no pricey professional development fees or expensive learning modules associated with promoting it. People who come in with this trait seem to hold onto it in the face of even the most adverse conditions. Despite abuse and humiliation, the teacher still clings to that love of literature or chemistry or calculus. Indeed, he may love it all the more for the difficulty and chaos around him. It's the fixed anchor in the storm, the one sure thing in the face of flux and change. Love of subject may not keep a teacher in the field indefinitely, but it seems to extend the amount of time it takes her to burn out. If you really, truly love American history, after all, there isn't much you can do besides teaching to actively engage with that subject every day.

The challenge, of course, is for schools to find these subject-loving teachers in the first place. Most public school systems do very little in the way of active recruiting. In my many years at Smith College I can count on the fingers of one hand the number of districts that contact our Education Department for student referrals. Rarely does a superintendent or a human resources coordinator come looking for top candidates to hire. And when they do, students are rarely asked to describe their intellectual passions or to talk about their subjects in ways that would demonstrate the kind of sustaining engagement I refer to in this essay. I know that if a superintendent asked for my opinion, I could say with confidence, "Meredith is an incredible young woman who loves English literature to the point of mania." I'd stake my life on the fact that Meredith will stay in the field. I wouldn't necessarily want to bet on the student who is entering teaching to save the world.

Chapter 5

Practitioner Inquiry and the Messy Reality of Classroom Practice

CURT DUDLEY-MARLING

A s I BEGAN WRITING THIS ESSAY I read a piece by Cary Tennis (2010), an advice columnist for Salon.com, linking the depressing political environment to Fox News, a consumerist culture, and a failing educational system. This casual reference to "a failing educational system" is emblematic of what is widely taken as common sense among the media, educational policy makers, and the American public: Public schools in the United States are failing to adequately educate our youth. Americans' ambivalence toward its schools is reflected in the most recent Phi Delta Kappa/Gallup annual poll of the public's attitudes toward the public schools. Reflecting a long-standing trend, Americans continue to express a low opinion of public schools in general, while ironically giving relatively high marks to their local schools (Bushaw & McNee, 2009). Presented with this finding, Secretary of Education Arne Duncan offered a particularly harsh evaluation of American schools:

> Too many people don't understand how bad their own schools are. They always think it's somebody else's kid who's not being educated. They don't understand that it's their own kid who's being shortchanged. That's part of our challenge. How do you awaken the public to believe that your own kid isn't getting what they need and you don't know it. . . . We need to wake them up. (Richardson, 2009, p. 29)

Although I am tempted to challenge Duncan's dubious claim about "how bad" American schools are (see Berliner & Biddle, 1995; Bracey, 2000; Rothstein, 1998 for evidence that, on balance, U.S. schools are doing reasonably well), there is little doubt that this sentiment animates current demands for reform of American education, reforms that largely situate school failure in the bodies of teachers and, to a lesser extent, in students and their families. School choice and other market-based reforms presume that only competition will inspire putatively uninspired teachers to teach well. Underlying high-stakes testing and merit pay, for instance, is the assumption that teachers need to be motivated through various rewards and sanctions to do what is best for their students. Even when teachers are sufficiently motivated, there are still doubts among reformers that teachers can be trusted to make the best decisions for their students. "Research-based" practice, a leitmotif of No Child Left Behind, is based on the belief that teachers need explicit guidance from distant researchers to identify best practices for teaching their students. Increasingly, these best practices are taking the form of prescriptive, teacher-proof, one-size-fits-all curricula, which insure that teachers do not deviate from these practices.

These various reform initiatives reveal educational reformers' low opinion of teachers who cannot be trusted to act in the best interests of their students. But what's even more striking to me is the simplistic assumptions about teaching and learning—and about the human experience in general—that underpin these reforms. One-size-fits-all prescriptions that emerge from high-stakes testing (see Nichols & Berliner, 2007) and research-based practice, for example, disregard potential variations in students' preferred learning styles and developmental differences among individual students in general. Merit pay schemes ignore the complex, uneven trajectory of human development as if learning proceeds in a predictable, linear fashion. Further, in the context of market-based reforms, successful teaching (and learning) is strictly a matter of individual responsibility (Harvey, 2005; Hursh, 2007), trumping poverty and discrimination, violence, underfunded schools, poor working conditions for teachers (including large class sizes), unmotivated students, and so on. From this perspective, schools can and should be reformed by straightforward policies that direct teachers to adopt more effective (read: "research-based") strategies while working harder to achieve success with their students.

This simple prescription ignores the complex reality of life in schools, as any teacher recognizes. The certain reality of educational reforms constructs teachers as technicians who are expected to deliver "research-based" practices to children who are treated as so many interchangeable widgets. Arguably, this construction of teaching and learning drains the humanity from teachers' work, robbing teachers of the pleasures of working with children (and their students of the pleasures of learning).

THE MESSY REALITY OF CLASSROOM PRACTICE

When I reviewed my evaluations for a graduate-level methods course I taught last semester, there was one student who expressed great frustration with me. She complained that whenever she asked me a question about what do to with a particular student in her class I would always qualify my response with "Well, it depends. . . ." It seems that she wanted certainty (i.e., strategies that work), but my response suggested that there are no certain solutions to student learning. To me, it depends on a student's linguistic and cultural background and background knowledge, her interests and developmental level, the teacher's style, the curriculum, and so on. To my "frustrated" student, my uncertainty was unacceptable, undermining any claims I might have had to "expert" status.

The obsession with "best methods" presumes that there are instructional strategies that work for all students and teachers, all of the time—or at least for most students and teachers, nearly all of the time. More to the point, the discourse of what works assumes that the conditions of learning—and learners themselves—are virtually identical across settings and therefore we should be able to predict with a high level of certainty that teaching and learning strategies that work with students in one classroom will work with other students in other classrooms. There are problems with the logic of these certain claims, however. First of all, certain claims of what works undergirded by "scientifically based" research are based on a fundamental misunderstanding of the meaning of quantitative models of research. Findings of "statistically significant differences" favoring particular instructional strategies lead to declarations that these strategies work. However, all that can reasonably be claimed based on these sorts of findings is that such strategies were more effective than other strategies to which they were compared on average. Strategies that are deemed to work are never found to work for all children, and the strategies to which they are compared are typically effective for at least some children. Put differently, there is always some uncertainty about the efficacy of instructional strategies that have been shown to work. This is a point to which I shall return shortly.

A more serious problem with certain claims about best methods (i.e, what works) is that such claims presume that classrooms are tidy, predictable spaces—a gross misrepresentation of life in real classrooms. Here's how Tom Newkirk (1992) put it:

> Teaching, closely read, is messy: full of conflict, fragmentation, and ambivalence. These conditions of uncertainty present a problem in a culture that tends to regard conflict as distasteful and that prizes unity, predictability, rational decisiveness, certainty. This is a setup: Teaching involves a lot of "bad" stuff, yet teachers are expected to be "good." (p. 21)

The problem for teachers is negotiating between the fiction of schools and classrooms as rational, predictable spaces and the messy, infinitely complex reality of life in real classrooms (Davis & Sumara, 2006; Dudley-Marling, 1997).

LIVING WITH UNCERTAINTIES, COMPLEXITIES, AND AMBIGUITIES

Prior to taking a position at Boston College I worked at York University in Toronto. During the 1991–92 academic year I took a leave from my professorial duties at York to teach third grade. It had been

13 years since I had worked in an elementary classroom, and I was losing confidence in my ability to work with teachers. Oddly, this was just a couple of years after I coauthored a very successful text on teaching struggling readers (Rhodes & Dudley-Marling, 1988). Still, the idea was to enhance my work with teachers by being more certain of what I knew about teaching. But this isn't how it worked out. Returning to the classroom did not make me more certain of my pedagogical knowledge. I do believe that this experience made me a more effective teacher educator; but reflecting on all the data I collected during my year back in the classroom, I was struck by the uncertainties, ambiguities, and complexities of life in my third-grade classroom. I learned firsthand the power of practitioner inquiry as a means of making sense of the complexities of teaching and learning. I also came to understand how "teaching stories that efface the messy reality of teaching reinforce the tyranny of certainty that limits the pleasure and self-satisfaction that teachers are able to derive from [their] work" (Dudley-Marling, 1997, p. xiii).

Acknowledging classrooms as complex systems (Davis & Sumara, 2006) requires a transformation of the work of teachers from technicians guided by distant researchers to thoughtful professionals who generate and interpret research findings and systematically reflect on their practice—all in the service of enhancing student learning. Further, constructing teaching as an intellectually engaging activity sustains teachers by affording them opportunities to make sense of the complexities of life in classrooms and, ultimately, to find pleasure in their work.

TEACHERS AS INTERPRETERS OF RESEARCH

Earlier, I made the point that research on what works indicates—at best—effective pedagogical practices for the mythical average student whose relationship to individual children is uncertain. Again, no instructional strategy is ever effective for all children, all of the time (Allington & Johnston, 2001; Pearson, 1997). "Proven" programs work in the hands of expert teachers who modify or alter them (or abandon them altogether) based on careful, ongoing assessment of the complex needs of individual learners (Allington, 2002). In other words, effective teachers do not blindly implement the agenda of distant researchers. They integrate their knowledge of research on classroom instruction with their professional knowledge, their experience, and their knowledge of their students to determine what is likely to be most effective for particular children. Chapman and Kinloch (in press) use the concept of "fittingness" to describe teachers' ability—as readers of research—to make connections between themselves and the studies they read and to transfer or translate the newly described situation to their own situations. As Chapman and Kinloch describe it,

> fittingness refers to the ability of the teacher, given that she has ample description and information about the contexts of the study, to then relate those contexts to her own, given that only she knows the details of that context. Only the reader, who knows both her context and the published study, can properly transfer the findings or suggestions to a new setting. It is incumbent upon the researcher to provide the necessary emic perspective to the reader so that she can properly make those transfers. (in press)

Teachers who do not—or cannot, in the case of prescribed curricula—exercise a significant measure of professional discretion in implementing research on effective classroom practices will find it difficult, perhaps impossible, to meet the individual needs of students in their classrooms (Allington, 2002). The simplistic notion that best practices readily generalize to all settings conflicts with the messy realities of teaching and learning in diverse classroom settings. As Gutiérrez, Baquedano-López, and Turner (1997) put it, "Even our most dear beliefs and practices are transformed in their enactment in classroom activity" (p. 372), reflecting the Davis and Sumara (2006) stance that classrooms are infinitely complex systems; therefore, the assumption that any instructional strategy can generalize from one classroom setting to another is always problematic. We must trust teachers to interpret research findings. It is, however, incumbent on teachers to reflect on the effectiveness of instruction with individual students as a matter of routine.

TEACHERS AS RESEARCHERS

Athaneses (in press) refers to what he calls "practice-based evidence," a notion that turns the construct of evidence-based practice on its head. Instead of teachers as mere recipients of knowledge generated by distant researchers—what Cochran-Smith and Lytle refer to as "knowledge-for-practice"—the idea of practice-based evidence positions teachers as "making their classrooms and schools sites for inquiry, connecting their work in schools to larger issues, and taking a critical perspective on the theory and research of others" (Cochran-Smith & Lytle, 1999, p. 273). As practitioner researchers, teachers engage in rigorous, systematic inquiry to consider research questions related to the complexity of life in classrooms, particularly student learning (Cochran-Smith & Lytle, 2009). When I taught third grade, for example, I asked a number of questions related to teaching and learning, including:

- How effective was I with my struggling readers?
- How were my students using reading and writing to build and maintain social relationships?
- Was I treating the boys and girls in my classroom equitably?
- What was an effective way to teach spelling?
- How could I use multicultural literature to acknowledge my students' cultural backgrounds? (For a detailed treatment of how I considered these questions, see Dudley-Marling, 1997.)

More recently, I have been approached by a third-grade teacher named Faythe Beauchemin who teaches in Belmont, Massachusetts, to work with her to examine the impact of inquiry on her students' learning. Specifically, Faythe wants to examine the effect of the inquiry projects in which her students engage on their learning and to see how she might improve the quality of these inquiry projects. This past fall, Faythe and I began collecting audio and video recordings, observational notes, student work samples, and interviews with students to examine the nature and impact of inquiry in her classroom. As we've begun to review the data we have collected in Faythe's classroom so far, Faythe has been able to see evidence of what students are learning through inquiry and how she might adjust her teaching to be even more effective, particularly with a few students who have been less active in inquiry groups.

TEACHING AS AN INTELLECTUAL ACTIVITY

According to the National Commission on Teaching and America's Future (NCTAF, 2007), up to 20% of new teachers leave the profession within 3 years. The attrition rate is even worse in urban schools, where perhaps 50% of new teachers leave teaching within 5 years. Data routinely collected at Boston College where I now teach indicate that nearly 10% of the students in our teacher preparation program never take a teaching position despite a degree in teacher education. Others transfer from teacher education to other programs in the School of Education. There is a range of reasons why teachers leave the classroom after just a few years (or do not enter the classroom at all), but clearly the pleasures of working with children and having a chance to influence their lives—the very reasons most teachers entered the profession—are often insufficient compensation for what is a very difficult job.

My own sense is that many teachers leave the profession because they find the work intellectually unsatisfying. As a nation, we claim that we want "the best and the brightest" teachers in our classrooms but, increasingly, the work of teachers, particularly teachers working in urban schools, is reduced to technical activity in which teachers and students engage in low-level, one-size-fits-all, scripted curricula. Scripted curricula dictate the scope, sequence, and pace of instruction and indicate what teachers are to say and do and when and which student responses are acceptable. Such practices grossly oversimplify the teaching and learning process, severely limiting the possibility for teachers to find intellectual satisfaction in their work. Faythe Beauchemin, the teacher with whom I will be collaborating to investigate the impact of inquiry in her classroom, is sustained by an intense intellectual curiosity that, combined with a commitment to do what is best for her students, makes her a superb teacher. Without opportunities to satisfy her intellectual curiosity it is doubtful that Faythe would remain in teaching for long. There are, I believe, lots of bright, thoughtful, and curious teachers just like Faythe, and like Faythe, many of these teachers stay in teaching because they work in schools that nurture and support their inquisitiveness. Other teachers find the intellectual tedium of prescriptive curricula impossible to endure and leave the profession after just a few years. Higher salaries and more effective induction programs are widely assumed to be the antidotes to high rates of teacher attrition, but I believe these incentives, while important, will be insufficient for retaining thoughtful, intellectually curious teachers. Ultimately, teaching is a job, not a calling, and to attract and retain the "best and brightest" it must include intellectual challenges as one of its compensations. Certainly for me, and for teachers like Faythe, the intellectual challenge is essential to sustaining a passion for teaching. Constructing teaching as intellectual work is also a way to inject thoughtfulness and rigor into the current debate about school reform from which the voices of teachers have been largely absent. The current state of educational reform, simply because it is detached from the reality of life in real schools and real classrooms, is doomed to failure. For the sake of our children—and the bright, thoughtful women and men who teach them—we need to create spaces in our schools for thoughtful, intellectually curious, and passionate teachers like Faythe.

REFERENCES

Allington, R. L. (2002). *Big brother and the national reading curriculum: How ideology trumped evidence.* Portsmouth, NH: Heinemann.

Allington, R. L., & Johnston, P. (2001). What do we know about effective fourth-grade teachers and their classrooms? In C. Roller (Ed.), *Learning to teach reading: Setting the research agenda* (pp. 150–165). Newark, DE: International Reading Association.

Athaneses, S. (in press). Research as praxis: Documenting the dialectical relationship between theory and practice. In D. Lapp & D. Fisher (Eds.), *Handbook of Research on Teaching the English Language Arts* (3rd ed.). New York: Taylor & Francis.

Berliner, D. C., & Biddle, B. J. (1995). *The manufactured crisis: Myths, fraud, and the attack on America's public schools.* Reading, MA: Addison-Wesley.

Bracey, G. (2000). The TIMSS "final year" study and report: A critique. *Educational Researcher, 29,* 4–10.

Bushaw, W. J., & McNee, J. A. (2009). The 41st annual Phi Delta Kappa/Gallup Poll of the public's attitudes toward the public schools. *Phi Delta Kappan, 91*(1), 8–23.

Chapman, T., & Kinloch, V. (in press). Emic perspectives of research. In D. Lapp & D. Fisher (Eds.), *Handbook of Research on Teaching the English Language Arts* (3rd ed.). New York: Taylor & Francis.

Cochran-Smith, M., & Lytle, S. L. (1999). Relationships of knowledge and practice: Teacher learning in community. *Review of Research in Education, 24,* 249–305.

Cochran-Smith, M., & Lytle, S. L. (2009). *Inquiry as stance: Practitioner research in the next generation.* New York: Teachers College Press.

Davis, B., & Sumara, D. (2006). *Complexity and education: Inquiries into learning, teaching, and research.* Mahwah, NJ: Erlbaum.

Dudley-Marling, C. (1997). *Living with uncertainty: The messy reality of classroom practice.* Portsmouth, NH: Heinemann.

Gutiérrez, K., Baquedano-López, P., & Turner, M. G. (1997). Putting language back into language arts: When the radical middle meets the third space. *Language Arts, 74,* 368–378.

Harvey, D. (2005). *A brief history of neoliberalism.* New York: Oxford University Press.

Hursh, D. (2007). Policies assessing No Child Left Behind and the rise of neoliberal education. *American Educational Research Journal, 44,* 493–518.

National Commission on Teaching and America's Future (NCTAF). (2007). *The high cost of teacher turnover.* Washington, DC: Author.

Newkirk, T. (1992). Silences in our teaching stories: What do we leave out and why? In T. Newkirk (Ed.), *Workshop 4: The teacher as researcher* (pp. 21–30). Portsmouth, NH: Heinemann.

Nichols, S. L., & Berliner, D. C. (2007). *Collateral damage: How high-stakes testing corrupts America's schools.* Cambridge, MA: Harvard Education Press.

Pearson, D. (1997). First grade studies: A personal reflection. *Reading Research Quarterly, 32,* 428–432.

Rhodes, L. K., & Dudley-Marling, C. (1988). *Readers and writers with a difference: A holistic approach to teaching learning disabled and remedial students.* Portsmouth, NH: Heinemann.

Richardson, J. (2009). Quality education is our moon shot. *Phi Delta Kappan, 91*(1), 24–29.

Rothstein, R. (1998). *The way we were? The myths and realities of America's student achievement.* A Century Foundation Report. New York: Century Foundation Press.

Tennis, C. (2010). Since you asked: My dad's become a crazed right winger. *Salon.com.* Retrieved May 19, 2010, from http://www.salon.com/life/since_you_asked/2010/05/19/right_wing_dad

Chapter 6

Burning Out in the Social Studies

JAMES W. LOEWEN

IN THE YEARS SINCE MY BOOK *Lies My Teacher Told Me* debuted in 1995 I must have spoken in front of 20,000 teachers of social studies and history. What have I learned? All kinds of tips and tricks on how to teach history more effectively, on the bright side. On the darker side, however, I've learned that teachers of history/social studies divide into two groups: those who teach creatively and those who don't. Unfortunately, I think the two categories divide about one-third and two-thirds. Students who languish under the second type spend more time with their textbooks than do students in any other subject.

This finding left me stunned at first. I would have thought maybe plane geometry. After all, how can students of plane geometry interview their folks about dodecahedrons? How can they use community resources? old folks? the census? the Web? books in the library? Yet social studies students can use all of these sources of information and more. The two-thirds of history teachers who just teach from the textbook are not happy. Some teach this way because they feel they must because their students face "objective," high-stakes exams, often associated with the No Child Left Behind Act. Most of these tests are in multiple-choice format to facilitate machine grading. Typically they are "twig tests"—not testing the forest for the trees, not even testing trees, but only the twigs—questions like "The Civil War began in (A) 1776, (B) 1860, (C) 1861, (D) 1961, or (E) all of the above." Teachers feel they must teach to these tests, not only so their pupils can pass them, but also because their students' scores are used to evaluate their own performance and that of their school. Teachers cannot know which minutiae will be on the test, so they have students read every mind-numbing page of their textbook, answer every question posed by each photo caption, review each "Theme," identify each "Central Issue," and understand each "Checking for Understanding" found in *The American Journey*, to take one recent textbook example.

Other teachers teach every page because they feel they should: Students paid cash money to rent their huge textbooks, now averaging 1,152 pages, or the state paid a huge sum to buy them, so students had better read them. *Journey* actually sets a new record for the tallest, widest, and heaviest American history textbook ever . . . and it's just for middle schoolers! Thus, just as one reason why the United States dropped the atomic bomb on Nagasaki was because we had it, one reason why history students spend so much time with their textbooks is because they have them. Having a bigger book only spurs conscientious teachers to get students to spend even more time with it. Another reason why many history and social studies teachers teach from the textbook is because this is how most of them were taught. They have not experienced role models who got them to go beyond or even challenge their textbooks. They just do what was done unto them.

Fear keeps some teachers on the straight-and-narrow, stick-to-the-textbook path. Teachers worry that if they get students thinking, they'll be seen as rocking the boat and might get in trouble with their principal, or perhaps with parents or some vague watchdog out there. The basic story line in American history textbooks is one of unending progress: We were discovered by great men, our nation had great founders, and we've been improving steadily ever since. Getting students to challenge their textbooks seems tantamount to undermining this story line and seems, in a word, unpatriotic.

Teachers may also worry that they do not know enough history to deviate from the book, which was written by a panel of expert historians, after all. They fear they might unleash a Pandora's box. If they were to have their students research a topic—the women's movement, the Korean War, whatever— their students might know more than they do about it. In turn, the teacher might lose face, perhaps even control. Teachers also worry that students might go off on tangents, relying on unvetted information from Web sites with religious, racial, or just plain ridiculous axes to grind.

Each of these causes for caution is understandable, yet none is a valid reason for clinging so tightly to the textbook. Huge textbooks may have been needed for students in small towns in bygone years, when neither the community library nor the high school library had many resources for teaching American history. Today, however, wherever students have access to telephone lines, they can browse hundreds of thousands of historic documents on the Web, see transcripts from oral histories taken across the United States, and read many books published before 1923 (and some later works). The Web liberates teachers to use the textbook as one of many teaching aids, and not necessarily the most important.

Pioneering new ways to teach, different from how we were taught, can be difficult. Nevertheless, just as courses in social studies and history that relied on the textbooks were probably not our favorites in our own K–12 years, nor are they popular today. Students learn more when they like and are interested in their courses. In turn, their interest keeps teachers in the game.

"Covering" the textbook allows no time to discover or uncover anything. No time to get excited. No time to "do" history because we are too busy "learning" it. Like their students, teachers wind up dreading history class, but since that's all they teach, their morale winds up even lower than their students'. Burnout looms. Driving a delivery van seems a happier alternative—at least people want to see their UPS person.

"Standardized" tests do constitute a problem, to be sure. The only real solution is to construct tests worth teaching to. Ironically, considering its source, such a test exists: the Advanced Placement exam in U.S. History. Its DBQs (Document-Based Questions) actually challenge students to write coherent essays that use (or ignore, as appropriate) historic documents. The thinking, writing, and background information required by the DBQ are skills also required by life after formal education. Never in the world of employment, checkbook balancing, or just plain citizenship do we have to choose among alternatives A, B, C, D, or E. Yet multiple-choice tests only prepare us to take multiple-choice tests.

Even if your students do face required multiple-choice exams that test twig history, however, the best way to get them to retain twigs is not by having them memorize twigs. Today's teenybopper has learned to cope with twig questions by devoting a certain mass of synapses to "useless facts in American history." As soon as the student has finished the exam on that unit, she clears that area of the brain to make room for more twigs. In June the synapses get cleared once more, and the student has retained nothing—yet earned an A! When we teach history as a series of important issues, on the other hand, each presented with passion and with relevance to the present, students invest intellectual and emotional energy in their work and remember things for years.

Teachers can try to persuade their school districts to adopt short paperback textbooks, which they can sell to students for less than the cost of renting the behemoths of yore. In districts locked into 1,150-page textbooks, teachers need not assign every page. Instead, teachers need to develop a list of 30 to 50 topics, each of which is important for understanding our nation's past. Each should excite the teacher; each should have relevance to the present. This list cannot be totally arbitrary. If it does not include the Civil War and its impact, it's not competent. If it does not include the making and use of the Constitution, it's a bad list. But it does not have to—indeed, it must not—cover everything. One teacher leaves out the national bank crisis during the Andrew Jackson administration; she does not know how to teach the bank crisis. Another omits the Korean War—simply omits it; he has not figured out the relevance of the Korean War to the present, other than to explain why the peninsula is divided. And the world does not come to an end! On the contrary, their classes convey to their teachers the excitement students feel about the 35 or 41 topics they do teach.

Fear of repercussions from parents or administrators turns out to be most widespread of all, but perhaps easiest to deal with. Experienced teachers have found ways to minimize or eliminate those repercussions. They link their list of topics to the various skills that their state says it wants to develop via its social sciences/history curriculum. One topic will cultivate students' ability to marshal evidence. Another will teach students the difference between primary and secondary sources. A third will help students learn to put documents in perspective, using the term *historiography*. Principals may only want about 10 minutes on all this, but those minutes are well spent. They bring on board an important ally who can help sell the new approach to doubting parents.

Students then use different methods to learn about each item. They may use a formal debate to examine the two (or more) sides of an issue. They may put a historic figure on trial. They may explore another topic on their own, via a written term paper. Interviewing diverse members of the community may provide the key to exploring yet another issue, for instance, the women's movement of the 1970s. And yes, the textbook, too, plays a role.

Although scary in prospect, teachers who have put such methods into practice report that they now look forward to their social sciences/history classes. Wonderful stories result—such as the sixth graders who wrote the publisher, complaining that their textbook completely left out the fact that most of our early presidents owned slaves—triggering a hilarious nonreply. Or the girls who entered their local history project into the National History Day competition and then changed how their town remembered the past on its historical markers.

What about the charge of being unpatriotic? Surely the American past is not so dreadful that we must lie about it and pretty it up. Surely we can face our blunders as well as our triumphs.

What about Pandora's Box? Teachers can simply make that problem disappear by redefining the situation: Students are our allies as we discover history together. Therefore, when students learn something we don't know, teachers can feel pride rather than worry.

What about the problem of questionable sources when going beyond the textbook? Teachers can make lemonade by asking students themselves to critique a particularly bad Web site. Moreover, teachers must not let students use only the Web to complete any assignment. We still have libraries, after all, with books in them. We still have newspapers, old people to interview, and census tables to understand. Indeed, we still have the whole panoply of information that historians and sociologists have always used. Precisely these sources have been placed off limits to students by courses that insisted on teaching history solely from the textbook.

Steadily growing is the proportion of teachers in social studies and history who teach creatively, who help their students challenge rather than simply "learn" their textbooks. If you're not already in this crew, come aboard! There is little to fear, except fear itself, to paraphrase . . . now, who was that guy?

REFERENCE

Loewen, J. W. (1995). *Lies my teacher told me: Everything your American history textbook got wrong.* New York: The New Press.

Chapter 7

Regrounded

SAM M. INTRATOR

A FTER 12 YEARS OF BEING a high school English teacher, I became a full-time teacher educator. While I relished the opportunity to work with college students and appreciated the time to work through scholarly endeavors, I also mourned the loss of my primary vocational identity: high school teacher. In truth, becoming a teacher educator involves not just a becoming, but also a leaving. Teacher educators still teach, but they teach about a context they no longer fully inhabit. And so there are times when I look out at my student teachers and feel like an outsider, a pretender—like a former athlete relegated to the broadcast booth to provide commentary on a game that I used to play. At my worst moments, I felt like a sham. At other times I felt as though I was working with hazy recollections of a past life. Children's book author Elizabeth Nesbitt said that when she was a child she used to "pray fervently, tearfully, that when I should be grown up I might never forget what I thought, felt, and suffered as a child." Nesbitt's refrain describes a fear that stalked my transition from K–12 practitioner to teacher educator: Would I forget about what I thought, felt, and suffered? Even if I did remember, would my archive of powerful memories suffice—especially since one of the first rules of teaching is to understand how the immediate context of a classroom, a school, and a community continually shifts and emerges?

I suspect my experience is not unique. The typical teacher educator comes from the K–12 setting: More than 80% of education faculty have had primary experience in elementary and secondary schools, typically around 10 years on average (Cochran-Smith & Zeichner, 2005; Ducharme & Ducharme, 1996; *RATE VIII*, 1995). While I began my stint in higher education determined to stay grounded, once inside the university milieu powerful forces began to work on me, and it was difficult to balance my commitments to the college and my desire to stay embedded in schools. These tensions are well documented. To begin with, teacher educators are expected to assume a range of professorial responsibilities that include research, teaching, service obligations, and collaboration across departments (Ducharme & Ducharme, 1995; Lunenberg, Korthagen, & Swennen, 2007). Furthermore, powerful status and hierarchy forces influence how we apportion our time and commitments to schools. On the one hand, teacher educators believe in the efficacy of working closely with schools, but they also perceive "an inverse relationship between professional prestige and the intensity of involvement with the formal education of teachers" (Lanier & Little, 1986, p. 530). The upshot of this is that I felt as though I were on a saltwater taffy machine—slowly being churned, stretched, wound, pulled, and spun. It was not comfortable and it took its toll.

Over the last 5 years, I have come inhabit this space more comfortably, and in doing so I believe I have reclaimed dimensions of my identity, my passion, and perhaps most important, my authenticity. My way forward begins with an idea best described in the *The Elements of Teaching* by Banner and Cannon (1997). They observe:

> The teachers whom we remember most vividly are those who knew their subjects best and transmitted them with the greatest intensity and love. They were confident in their knowledge, and not dogmatic; they acted out their own struggles to understand in front of us, joyful when they understood something fresh, troubled when they did not or could not know. They joined us at the laboratory bench, in the library, at the museum, puzzling with us over a test tube result, complaining about a book's interpretation, discovering a painting's meaning. They stood before us to present the act of learning with a sort of honesty that we rarely encounter in everyday life. It is such examples

of passion and exhilaration that students need in their teachers. Only in that way can students meet the importunate demands of learning with a full heart; only then can their thirst for learning move them on. (pp. 15–16)

Since I began my work as a teacher educator, I felt as if I had left the workbench. I needed to find a way back. One of my dearest friends and colleagues, Rob Kunzman, helped me find my way. Rob and I taught high school together and we both left teaching to become teacher educators. We talked often of the gap and how different the world of teacher education was from our old lives. Rob started to coteach an English class at a local high school. I went to visit him at the high school and watched him work with his high school class. It was inspiring.

I returned home determined to follow Rob's lead. My way back home involved cofounding Project Coach—a full-service, out-of-school program where I teach high school and middle school students to be sport coaches and then work alongside them to run youth sport leagues for elementary-age youth in underserved neighborhoods in their own community. The program's premise is that sport coaches must employ a complex repertoire of dynamic and authentic leadership skills, behaviors, and aptitudes. Coaching is merely a vehicle to teach and practice key achievement skills such as communications, initiative-taking, perseverance, conflict resolution, and other capacities that matter. I am fully invested and absorbed in the teaching that I do in Project Coach. It provides me the opportunity to teach, to mentor, to develop curriculum, to work shoulder-to-shoulder with youth and my student teachers. We work with vulnerable populations, so it is hard and demanding work, but in its best moments I feel vital and authentic.

Rob and I continue to write and think about how to structure our work in the academy so that we can more seamlessly bridge and connect our two worlds. We have written about it as *grounded practice,* an approach whereby teacher educators not only teach university-based classes but also extend their practice to the K–12 setting with K–12 students (Intrator & Kunzman, 2009). Our intent was to think beyond the idea of division and imagine a "lab bench" where university-based teacher educators, student teachers, K–12 practitioners, and—most important—K–12 students are present and engaged in teaching and learning.

The poet David Whyte has written that work is where "we can make ourselves; work is where we can break ourselves" (2002, p. 12). I also think work is where we can lose ourselves, and it is where we can find ourselves. I believe there is an ongoing, ever-shifting relationship between the self and our work. My journey into higher education demanded that I renegotiate my sense of vocation. I was definitely searching for what Rob and I have written about as *vocational vitality*, a quality of presence that includes an engrossment in one's work marked by a sense of dedication to the belief that the work is meaningful and purposeful (Intrator & Kunzman, 2006). It involves a commitment to one's labors that organizational theorist William Kahn (1992) described as being "fully there"—a psychological and experiential presence that allows an individual to infuse his role and task performances with a sense of personhood. I am a teacher, but the context of my teaching matters.

In the end, regrounding in the K–12 setting enabled me to reclaim a sense of vocational vitality. I feel more absorbed in the central action of my work. I no longer reside merely in the broadcast booth, but I participate, albeit in a modified fashion. Not only do I feel more comfortable with my work, but I also believe that my expanded role enables me to be a better teacher educator because my knowledge is no longer distant or abstract. In the end, I don't mean to hold up my own efforts as an ideal to be replicated, but as an illustration of my personal effort to renew my own practice and to keep myself engaged.

REFERENCES

Banner, J. M., & Cannon, H. C. (1997). *The elements of teaching*. New Haven: Yale University Press.

Cochran-Smith, M., & Zeichner, K. M. (2005). *Studying teacher education: The report of the AERA panel on research and teacher education.* Mahwah, NJ: Erlbaum.

Ducharme, E. R., & Ducharme, M. (1995). Development of the teacher education professoriate. In F. B. Murray & American Association of Colleges for Teacher Education (Eds.), *The teacher educator's handbook: Building a knowledge base for the preparation of teachers* (pp. 691–714). San Francisco: Jossey-Bass.

Ducharme, M., & Ducharme, E. R. (1996). A study of teacher educators: Research from the USA. *Journal of Education for Teaching, 22*(1), 57–70.

Intrator, S. M., & Kunzman, R. (2006). The person in the profession: Renewing teacher vitality through professional development. *The Educational Forum, 71*(1), 16–33.

Intrator, S. M., & Kunzman, R. (2009). Grounded: Practicing what we preach. *Journal of Teacher Education, 60*(5), 512–519.

Kahn, W. A. (1992). To be fully there: Psychological presence at work. *Human Relations, 45*(4), 321–349.

Lanier, J. E., & Little, J. W. (1986). Research on teacher education. In M. Wittrock (Ed.), *Handbook of research on teaching* (3rd ed., pp. 527–569). New York: Macmillan.

Lunenberg, M., Korthagen, F., & Swennen, A. (2007). The teacher educator as a role model. *Teaching and Teacher Education: An International Journal of Research and Studies, 23*(5), 586–601.

RATE VIII: Teaching teachers—relationships with the world of practice. (1995). Washington, DC: American Association of Colleges for Teacher Education.

Whyte, D. (2002). *Crossing the unknown sea: Work as a pilgrimage of identity.* Riverhead Books: New York.

Chapter 8

Open Doors

LINDA NATHAN

Richard stands in front of his math poster titled "The Parabola of the Fugue" in a crowded assembly hall with at least 50 other students who are also presenting today. Another 50 students are seated in front of the posters listening intently to their peers and writing comments and critiques of individual presentations. This is Math Fair day at Boston Arts Academy. Richard wipes his damp forehead with a handkerchief and nervously fingers the saxophone cord around his neck, which falls against the large gold chain and cross he also wears around his neck. He straightens the vest he wears over his pressed, button-down shirt. His fashion statement today is a mix of hip-hop and church attire. He stumbles a bit as he begins his presentation to his two peer reviewers, who are not in his math class, and another guest.

> G-good morning. My name is Richard and I'm a junior music major at Boston Arts Academy. In math class we have been studying quadratic equations, and the assignment was "What does art look like if a parabola inspires it?" I didn't know what to do for this project at first. We were told to create an original piece of work inspired by a quadratic function. I love music and so I composed a fugue. Bach wrote a lot of fugues in the Baroque era. My fugue has a four-part melody that repeats itself in different ways and for different instruments. You can see the piano line here and the saxophone line here. There's also a clarinet part and a flute. The melody, or the subject, is repeated in a specific way throughout the piece. Here you can

see how the notes form a parabola. I composed it that way on purpose. So here is my parabola and the quadratic equation for it. Here's the vertex and the roots, and you can see it doesn't cross the x-axis. Here's my in-out table. When you look at my music composition, you see the parabola. It's not a straight line. That would be a different equation. Do you have any questions?

One student reviewer stops writing on his peer review form and asks, "Where else do you see parabolas outside of math class?" Richard easily answers: "A mountain or a bridge can be in the form of a parabola, but so can pitch and tempo . . . that's what I'm working on here for this piece."

Richard makes intriguing connections between art and academics, and he is proud of his work. And we at Boston Arts Academy (BAA) are proud that there is a school to honor and support Richard's academic, artistic, and social-emotional growth. We have seen Richard in other academic classes. He struggles to read fluently and easily. His test scores are below average for his grade level, and he has an Individualized Education Plan that ensures he will get support from a special education teacher for his academic classes. He could have easily given up on school. And we all know that too many books have been written about the crisis of African American males, like Richard, who have given up on school.

Richard is also a large young man. He could be considered "intimidating" by some adults. He walks with a swagger, and his fashion sense mirrors that of current hip-hop artists with baggy pants and lots of bling around his neck. Although he is frustrated by the fact that he had to retake the MCAS (the Massachusetts high-stakes graduation test) for the third time, he balances that anger with his desire to perform well in his chamber group. He is on time for rehearsals and spends as much time as he can in the practice room or the computer MIDI lab working on compositions like this fugue. He loves classical music and at a recent professional concert of chamber music, I watched as he was entranced by the sounds and swayed to the melodies.

Richard also spends a period a day in the Learning Center, where he receives academic support for humanities, math, or science projects. At BAA Richard is a success story. True, he will not immediately enter a competitive 4-year college, but he will go to college, and he will finish. He will pursue his love of music, as he plans to major in music production and business so that he can open his own business one day. Richard is one of the reasons that Boston Arts Academy, a public high school in Boston Public Schools, exists.

Teddy is different. He is one of the most frustrating students I have ever taught. He was in my writing class for an entire year at BAA, and I couldn't get him to do anything. Writing is central to our curriculum. It begins in ninth grade with the theme of Identity, and all students create an Identity box and write a memoir. Even students who hate writing about themselves or being reflective usually find something in this term-long project that engages them. I have had students explore their love of racing cars or listening to heavy metal bands or caring for pets. A few students are even eager to delve into deeply personal material like the loss of a parent or a sibling, but there is no judgment about the level of personal information required in the memoir. We are teaching students to use vivid descriptive language, correct grammar, and good paragraph and essay structure, rather than psychoanalyzing the events in their lives.

But no matter what the assignment, Teddy resisted writing. He resisted almost as sport, but with such a passion that it was painful to watch. At times he would resort to banging his head on the desk, moaning in a way that distracted everyone, "I can't write. I have nothing to write. This is soooo boring!" I tried to put Teddy into a small group of students who were his friends, but he distracted them, too. I tried to work with him one-on-one or with a student teacher, but nothing seemed to work.

The sad part of all this is that Teddy is a fairly skilled student. He is excellent in math, memorizes easily, loves historical facts, and is devoted to music, but simply hates writing. No writing assignment all year engaged him. He hated writing about himself in the first-term memoir assignment; writing a research paper on an artist of the student's choice during second term was equally painful; and writing a compare-and-contrast essay during third term was torture. I felt that I could never engage him—neither one-on-one, nor in a small group. Teddy seemed to use all his energy to resist enjoying even the most engaging writing activities.

Sadly, as a veteran teacher, I had to admit that I wasn't going to make headway with Teddy. I couldn't sacrifice everyone else in the class to address Teddy's refusal to participate. Although I tried as often as possible to have Teddy work one-on-one with an aide, student teacher, or tutor, some days when there was no one available, I just let him be. The class, and I, needed a break. Occasionally, when his refusals to write became too boisterous and I couldn't isolate him one-on-one, I had to ask him to leave. This was sort of amusing since it meant he was sent to the office, but since both Ms. Torres, our coheadmaster, and I were teaching writing, no one but the secretary was there. For some reason, however, Teddy never messed with her. It was far from an ideal arrangement. There were family conferences; there were individual conferences; there were conferences with our counselor; there were learning contracts; there were behavioral contracts. Not much progress was made. Teddy hated to write. Writing class was about writing.

One day I watched him in his music class. It was a listening class; students wrote their observations about the music into their journals and then discussed their comments together. Teddy participated in the discussions. However, with some relief, I noticed that he didn't write in this class either. He participated in the discussions, but by the end of class he had written only a line or two.

In May, at Teddy's recital evening, I watched intently as he walked on the stage with his ensemble of eight other guitarists. His hair was combed. He was dressed neatly. I couldn't be sure that this was the same boy I taught in writing. Usually Teddy donned the torn and patched jean look with the high boots, studded jean jacket, and chains, if the security personnel hadn't confiscated them. I wouldn't have described him as dirty, but he certainly was never trying to look clean or well dressed. Yet when Teddy entered the stage of the Berklee College of Music Recital Hall, he looked like a handsome grown man. I did a double-take. Then the music started.

I was embarrassed at the way I kept looking at Teddy. He seemed possessed by the music, transported to another place. He kept time beautifully with his ensemble. When he soloed, his fingers nimbly plucked the strings, and chord changes seemed effortless. The piece ended and I noticed that his entire family was there—grandparents, parents, sisters—all clapping loudly. I wanted to give Teddy a standing ovation. I loved seeing him so engaged, seeing the music work its magic. I felt that Teddy had given me a great gift as a teacher. I would have another year to figure out how to engage him in writing. I had seen him engage. I knew it was possible, completely possible. Now, together, we would figure out how to make writing flow like music.

Boston Arts Academy, which opened its doors in 1998 as Boston's first public high school for the visual and performing arts, grew out of the vision and hard work of six private and public colleges in Massachusetts. From the onset, BAA's mission was quite different. From the moment students attend our intensive one-week summer orientation prior to freshman year, they learn and come to believe that they will graduate from BAA and they will have productive futures after graduation. These futures may include college, a professional track like a dance company or a hairdressing school, an apprenticeship as a plumber or the military. The point is that they will be prepared for life beyond high school. Although devoted to the arts, we believe a BAA education can be the best preparation not only for a career in the arts but also for a wide range of postsecondary options.

Reflecting the demographics of other urban schools, our student body is approximately 55% African American, 15% White, 27% Latino, and 3% Asian. About 65% of our students qualify for free or reduced-price lunch, a federal indicator of poverty. Gender ratios are 60% female and 40% male students, which is consistent with art schools across the country, and approximately 15% of our students receive special education services ranging from mild to moderate. What makes our demographics different from other large Boston high schools is the higher percentage of White students and the lower percentage of students eligible for free or reduced lunch. Thus we are both a racially and socioeconomically diverse school.

Another critical difference is that our students audition for one of 400 spots, and with the help of college admissions colleagues we have become fairly proficient in judging whether a student can and will sustain and enjoy 2–3 hours of arts classes a day in her chosen field. Potential music students must rank on a scale from 1-10 (10 is the highest) the importance of music in their lives; professing a love for the arts is a first step toward committing to living the arts. In dance auditions we look for bodies that move to a rhythm on the recording. In theater we look for flexibility requiring students to perform a monologue or a short scene in pairs. In visual arts, our students must be able to look out a window, paint what they see, and fill the page.

In our first twelve years we have graduated approximately 650 students, 95% of whom have gone on to college compared to 50% across the district. About 30% attend "arts" schools; others attend professional schools like Julliard or join dance companies like Alvin Ailey. Still others attend the University of Massachusetts in Boston, while some compete for prestigious scholarships at universities and colleges like Boston University, Brown, or Bard. On average, our students, African American and Latino students in particular, outperform their district and state peers, achieving at higher levels. High achievement scores have earned us "Breaking Ranks," a particularly prestigious award from the National Association of Secondary School Principals that acknowledges outstanding student achievement in "high poverty" and "high minority" schools. Our school also received the National School Library Media Program of the Year Award from the American Association of School Librarians (AASL) for our outstanding secondary school library program; this was one of the first times in the award's history that an urban secondary school has received such an accolade.

What fuels our passions? What keeps the arts and the dreams and goals of our students afire? Our mission, for one, but without committed faculty burned in to the belief that we can improve the lives of all students, mission is simply rhetoric. Of approximately 60 full- and part-time faculty in the school, 24% are African American, 17% are Latino, 9% are Asian, and the other 50% are White. Like their students they are inspired by the arts, content, pedagogy, students, and each other. More than half are first-generation college graduates and speak a native language other than English. Nearly all (95%) have master's degrees, and some more than one. Some are Boston Public School veterans—a few even graduated from Boston schools—but most are from around the country and even the world. Highly educated, dedicated, talented, and extraordinarily diverse, these teachers are strong-minded and strong-willed, but they are united in their desire to improve education for urban young people. This does not mean that there is always agreement about how, when, or what to improve—far from it—but this diversity engenders more ways and more reasons to enter into difficult conversations about race, class, gender, language, and culture. Unanimity of purpose, genuine belief in mission, a deep reverance for teaching and learning, and genuine respect for students, parents, and colleagues energize our school community and alight our passion.

True, not all schools can audition their students, choose their faculty, and provide explicit venues that allow teachers to collaborate and plan instruction centered on the "whole child," but all schools can develop an authentic mission grounded in theme, whether it be the arts, technology, science, media, or health. When schools stand for something unique or special they move beyond being "just a comprehensive high school." Art is transformative; it can change the alienation our students feel into affirmation and acceptance. That our young people, especially in urban schools, might never experience art-making at the secondary level is a travesty, but art is not enough. François-Auguste-René Rodin observed that, "The artist must create a spark before he can make a fire and before art is born, the artist must be ready to be consumed by the fire of his own creation." Sparks that ignite fires that nurture, sustain, and consume the student's creative spirit can only thrive in schools that are communities to which all students, teachers, and parents want to belong, communities in which all are artists of sorts, and communities into which the highest expectations and undying passion for teaching and learning are "burned in" to all its members. Only then will schools become places of radical transformation and places of the highest art!

Chapter 9

Fire and Water: Reflections on Teaching in the City

GREGORY MICHIE

I'M NOT SURE I EVER HAD THE FIRE TO TEACH. That's probably not the best way to begin, but don't misunderstand: I was passionate about my work. I taught seventh and eighth graders for a decade on the South Side of Chicago, and I did my best to be a thoughtful, creative, and dedicated educator. But I didn't teach like my hair was on fire, as one currently popular book recommends. It's a catchy image, sure, but it's not an approach that will work for everybody, and it definitely wasn't my style. If you interviewed my former students, I doubt any of them would describe me as being "on fire" or "fired up" about my work. I think they'd say I was devoted to it, though, and that I cared deeply about their learning and their lives in my own, noncombustible way.

My wife would say that, as a person, I'm more water than fire, and she's probably right. Thinking back, many of the teaching metaphors that have resonated with me most strongly have been water-related. I remember during my early years in the classroom saying that I felt like I was drowning, or that I was trying to keep my head above water (one of my favorite songs at the time, which I always thought spoke to my work as a teacher, was "Tread Water" by De La Soul). As I gained more experience, I paid more attention to the "flow" of my classes and my day. And I often compared teaching in city schools to swimming in an ocean's undertow: trying to hold onto a student-centered vision of education when so much of the school environment dragged you in a different, more mechanized direction.

So, yeah, I'm more water than fire. But that doesn't mean I didn't wrestle with the question of how to keep on keeping on as a teacher. Rivers can run dry. Raindrops evaporate. Like most teachers I know, I had to find ways to stay invigorated in the classroom, to fight off feelings of frustration and despair, to come back ready for another try on Tuesday when I had spent Monday just trying to stay afloat.

One of the things that kept me energized during my first few years was holding onto the belief that, with a mixture of patience, perseverance, and hard work, I could somehow close the gap. No, not the achievement gap. Important as that is to keep in view, the gap I had an eye on at the time was a different one: the distance between the sort of classroom I envisioned in my mind and the one I actually stepped into each morning. It was, on many days, a yawning, gaping chasm.

In the classroom I dreamed of, the curriculum was cocreated with my students, propelled by their questions and experiences but still connected to the "classical" knowledge they'd need to navigate the world beyond their neighborhood. The space hummed with activity, as small groups of kids collaborated on a variety of multilayered projects. Other students eagerly explored individualized topics of interest. Kids' voices were heard and valued, their minds were stretched and challenged, and each child felt affirmed as part of a supportive classroom community.

Then I woke up.

In my actual classroom full of real 13- and 14-year-olds, I often failed to engage my students in anything that might shake them out of the predictable routine we called school. If my plans started to unravel, I sometimes resorted to using the same deadening techniques I'd seen other teachers employ: demanding silence (and usually not getting it), passing out mindless worksheets, lecturing the kids about how disappointed I was in them. Teaching, as I did, in buildings where "the pedagogy of poverty" was in widespread use, I too often found myself surrendering to a misguided quest for control, all the while losing sight of the larger purposes of my work.

Occasionally, though, I did catch glimpses of the classroom I'd imagined. During my first year, a group of my students orchestrated a mock trial, in which they charged the school with discriminatory practices: While teachers were allowed to bring drinks into the school's unair-conditioned classrooms on hot days, students weren't. To make matters worse, a two-tiered menu existed in the lunchroom: one for students, and another, tastier one for adults. Had it been up to me, I would have probably chosen what I thought was a more "important" issue for the trial—police brutality, say, or disinvestment in the local community—but to my students, the food-and-drink double standards were immediate and real injustices, and the intensity and spark they brought to the mock trial were genuine. It was one of the few times that first year I could point to something that transpired in my classroom and say, "There. That's how I think school should be."

I held onto moments like the trial as testaments to what was possible in my classroom. As years went by they happened more frequently, but never as often as they had in the classroom I dreamed of creating. It was a constant ebb and flow—good days and bad, ordinary lessons and inspired ones, kids engaged one moment and distracted the next. Still, keeping an eye on that imagined classroom, inching toward the kind of education I knew my students deserved, was part of what kept me going when things got toughest, even if I doubted I'd ever get there completely.

* * * *

AT SOME POINT DURING MY FIRST FEW YEARS as a teacher, my mother, who lives in North Carolina, mailed me a card to encourage me in my work. I don't recall if it was in response to a particular incident I'd told her about or if it was just one of those random kindnesses of hers, but whatever prompted it, I kept the card taped to my refrigerator for many years. On the front was a quote from Thomas Merton. It captured an idea I'd thought about a lot in relation to my teaching, but hadn't quite been able to put into words.

Do not depend on the hope of results. When you are doing
the sort of work you have taken on . . . you may have to face
the fact that your work will be apparently worthless and even
achieve no result at all, if not perhaps opposite to what you expect. As you get used to this idea, you start more and more to
concentrate not on the results but on the value, the rightness,
the truth of the work itself. . . . [G]radually you struggle less
and less for an idea and more and more for specific people. . . .
In the end, it is the reality of personal relationships that saves
everything.

In the current educational climate, of course, Merton's words
sound hollow, if not naive. Results, usually in the form of standardized test scores, are all that seem to matter these days. Personal
relationships? Too touchy-feely in the era of corporate-style reform,
No Child Left Behind, and Race to the Top. We're repeatedly reminded that our success or failure as teachers is all about results,
test scores, the bottom line.

As much as I despise standardized tests, I wasn't unconcerned
with outcomes as a teacher. I understood, for example, that higher
test scores were an entry ticket in many ways for the kids I taught,
and I was happy (and, to be honest, often relieved) when my students' scores increased. But more than that, I wanted good things
for my students beyond the narrow bandwidth measured by a single
exam. I tried to help them develop tools for making sound decisions
in their lives, and I was thrilled when something turned out well
for any one of them.

But results weren't what kept me going as a teacher. They
couldn't have. Things often didn't play out the way I'd envisioned,
and if I'd pinned my hopes to attaining only "superior" outcomes—
especially as narrowly defined by test scores—I probably wouldn't
have lasted long. Some might say that's caving in to low expectations, but I don't think so. I'd say it's acknowledging the reality that
a single teacher can't change everything. Even when you do make
a difference in a kid's life, you don't always know you've done so.
Some things in teaching you just have to take on faith.

I'm reminded of a group of volunteers who run a turtle protection program in Holden Beach, a coastal town in North Carolina that my family sometimes visits. For hundreds of years, loggerhead turtles nested there without assistance, but due to pollution, poachers, and coastal development they've become an endangered species. So the volunteers, mostly retirees, have organized to help give the baby turtles a fighting chance. They build screens to protect the nests of eggs from raccoons and other scavengers. If eggs are laid in a spot that is susceptible to erosion, they carefully transport them to a safer location. And on nights when a nest "boils" and up to 120 hatchlings come squirming out, the volunteers are there, too, flashlights in hand. The turtles' instinct tells them to crawl toward the brightest horizon—the white foam of the breaking waves—but lights from beach houses can confuse them and send them off in the wrong direction. To make sure that doesn't happen, a volunteer stands ankle-deep in the ocean, shining a flashlight on the water as an extra guide. Other volunteers, as many as 15 or so, line a path to the surf, making sure the hatchlings don't get sidetracked.

I've watched this drama unfold, witnessed the tiny turtles scurrying down the sand toward the ocean, and while I'm sure the volunteers hope for the best for each of the newborns, the reality is that they never know the results of their patient, steady efforts. My guess is that, as Merton suggests, they focus instead on the value, the rightness of the work itself. As a teacher, I tried to do the same.

Of course, the saving grace, always, was the kids themselves. As Merton expresses so eloquently, it's personal relationships, in the end, that make most everything worthwhile. To be sure, plenty of other important matters demanded my attention in the classroom as well: what I should teach, how I should teach it, how I could create an affirming learning environment, how I could keep an eye on the larger contexts of my work. But none of those meant much, I learned, unless they were informed by strong, mutually respectful relationships with my students.

That's not to say that my relationships with the kids I taught weren't sometimes maddening or contentious, or that my efforts to make connections with students were always successful. Robbie, a seventh grader I taught toward the end of my time in the classroom, was being heavily recruited by the neighborhood gang, and in my reading class I saw him drifting slowly away. I tried to draw him back in, inviting him to stay after school to listen to CDs in my room, talking with his mom to get insight on what was happening at home, loaning him a book I thought he'd like, and taking him and a friend to browse at a nearby music store.

It seemed to be helping, until one morning before school a radio news broadcast I was only half listening to suddenly had me frozen: "Double murder last night . . . 14- and 15-year old are dead . . . teenager in custody . . . police say it could be gang related." The address the announcer gave for the crime wasn't far from my school, and when I heard it I felt my stomach tighten. I was worried that one of my students might have been killed. When I arrived at school a few minutes later, a colleague filled me in on the details. Indeed, two young men from the neighborhood had been shot dead. Robbie had been arrested for their murders.

That may seem like an unusual story to share. After all, wouldn't a tragic episode like that push someone away from teaching rather than keep them in it? You might think so, but if a big part of what's keeping you there are the relationships you've built, it doesn't work that way. Because even after a horrific, unimaginable event such as what happened with Robbie, life goes on for your students. So, later that morning in my third-floor classroom, I found myself sitting quietly with Robbie's classmates, feeling the weight of his empty chair, not knowing what to say, or how to make it better, but sensing that being together in the silence was, at that point, the most any of us could do. The next week, one of my colleagues organized students to write cards and collect donations for the families and friends of the two teens who had been killed. The kids in my reading class, knowing Robbie's 13th birthday was approaching, made him a giant card, and a few wrote individual letters to let him know they were thinking about him. I dropped everything off to him at the juvenile detention center a few nights later. We didn't have much of a conversation, but again, it seemed like the important thing was being there. I remember him smiling when he read the card.

It wasn't one of those moments you see in movies about teachers—the ones that, even if you know better, make you want to stand up and cheer. But it's part of the ebb and flow of real life in classrooms. Joy and heartbreak, tedium and excitement, flashes of inspiration, and moments of darkest doubt—all carrying you along for parts of the teaching journey, pushing you onward and drawing you back again.

Chapter 10

The Believing Game

PETER ELBOW

BURNED OUT AS DOUBT

WHEN WE FEEL BURNED OUT AS TEACHERS, it's easy to see the naiveté in some of the convictions that fueled us when we started out. Consider this common one: "I can improve the world by being a teacher." It becomes very hard to maintain this belief when we see too many students who don't give a damn, a society that doesn't seem to value teachers, a system that seems to work against our efforts, and worst of all, all our failures. My argument in this chapter is that it's not so feasible to really believe that naive idea, but it's absolutely feasible and productive to *try very hard to believe it*. I'm arguing that doing so involves something intellectually sophisticated—using what I call *the believing game*.

DEFINITIONS

I can define *the believing game* most easily and clearly by contrasting it with the *doubting game*. Indeed, the believing game derives from the doubting game. The *doubting game* represents the kind of thinking most widely honored and taught in our culture. It's sometimes called *critical thinking*. It's the disciplined practice of trying to be as skeptical and analytical as possible with every idea we encounter. By trying hard to doubt ideas, we can discover hidden contradictions, bad reasoning, or other weaknesses in them—especially in the case of ideas that seem true or attractive. We are using doubting as a tool for scrutinizing and testing ideas.

In contrast, the *believing game* is the disciplined practice of trying to be as welcoming or accepting as possible to every idea we encounter: not just listening to views different from our own and holding back from arguing with them; not just trying to restate them without bias (as Carl Rogers advocated); but actually trying to believe them. We are using believing as a different tool for scrutinizing and testing ideas. But instead of doubting in order to scrutinize fashionable or widely accepted ideas for hidden flaws, we use belief to scrutinize unfashionable or even repellent ideas for hidden virtues. Often we cannot see what's good in someone else's idea (or in our own!) until we work at believing it. When an idea goes against current assumptions and beliefs, or if it seems alien, dangerous, or poorly formulated, we often cannot see any merit in it.

A SHORT, IDEALIZED HISTORY OF BELIEVING AND DOUBTING

Believing seems to come first. It looks as though it was evolutionarily useful for children to believe parents and others with authority. When I was very little, my older brother and sister held out a spoonful of horseradish and said, "Here. This is good." I swallowed. After that, I wanted to distrust everything they told me, but soon I reverted to my natural trust and faith in them. That is, I tried for systematic doubt but failed.

Swallowing what looks good is a deep habit. Unless people are vigorously trained in critical thinking, they tend to grow up into adults who have a propensity to believe what looks obvious or what they hear from people in authority or from the culture. Adults, not just children, used to assume that a rain dance could make it rain; they used to burn witches because of disease outbreaks. And plenty of people still respond gullibly to e-mails saying they've won hundreds of thousands of dollars if they'll just send one thousand dollars for legal fees.

So human credulity gets us into trouble. But when some people get burned enough, they finally learn to doubt everything. We see this most nakedly in matters of the heart: some people who feel betrayed come to resist any close attachment. Sadly, we've been living through an era that tempts us into blanket cynicism. When we get burned out, we find ourselves doubting whether we're doing any good at all. Burned-out teachers often see cheating and plagiarism where it doesn't exist.

But if we stop to think for a moment, we realize that in fact we are not thinking carefully if we doubt everything. For we are inheritors of a more sophisticated kind of skepticism that has developed over the centuries. This is a tradition of systematic skepticism that I call *the doubting game* or methodological doubting. The goal is not to reject everything but to use skepticism as a test to see which ideas are more worthy of trust.

Socrates was in on the development of logic and he showed the outlines of this systematic use of doubting in his adversarial dialogues (and note a recurrent playful or "game" element in those dialogues). He usually fueled these conversations with skeptical questions: "But why is it good to obey our parents, our rulers, and our traditions?" He spurred young people to question skeptically what their elders and their culture told them to believe. But he wasn't trying to kill all belief—just to examine tempting beliefs with dialogic skeptical questioning. (He was killed for his efforts.)

Descartes is famous for a more self-consciously formal version of methodological doubting. He said, "I will doubt *everything*." But his goal was not to reject everything; his burning hunger was to find something he could believe—something that survived the test of doubting. Finally, with so-called Enlightenment thinking of the eighteenth century, with people like Voltaire undermining all religious authority, a lot of this kind of skeptical rationality became fairly orthodox. And there was an important social dimension to Enlightenment rationality. J. S. Mill gave the classic celebration of debate and argument: If we avoid censorship and create a truly free forum for the open debate of all ideas, he argues, we can winnow out bad thinking and find ideas that bear trust.

Note the important difference between blanket, naive, unthoughtful skepticism that rejects everything and the use of doubting as a methodological tool where the goal is not to reject but to test in order to see what's more trustworthy. Only temperamental skeptics are good at instinctive skepticism, but when a practice gets formulated as a tool—and we teach it as a conscious method in schools—then it's available to people of all temperaments.

Methodological doubting is central to the classical definition of *scientific method*: the process of trying to formulate various hypotheses about some particular issue in order to try to disprove those hypotheses and thereby see which ones seem to survive. The incredible success of science has given powerful authority to the idea of methodological or systematic doubting. Scientific knowledge has garnered incredible authority in our culture because of the accomplishments of technology. The principle has become enshrined: We can advance knowledge if we try to doubt and disprove what we're tempted to believe. For example, many people have faith in certain drugs or herbs that give them great relief, but scientifically double-blind experiments show that many of these particular drugs don't in themselves do the job. (I know, things are not quite as simple as the classic story of scientific method. I'll acknowledge that later.)

So this is where we are. We honor systematic skepticism or the doubting game as the best form of thinking. It's easy to doubt what's dubious, but the whole point of systematic skeptism is to try to doubt what we find most obvious or true or right. We can't act—or even think very far—unless we accept at least some view, so we want to know which views are most worthy of trust. Scientists do their best to disprove a hypothesis not because they want to reject it but in order to see if they can show it is worth trusting—for a while, anyway.

Let me continue this story briefly into the future. Note the progression so far: Naive believing causes trouble, so this leads us to doubt. But total blanket rejecting is too blunt a tool—and not livable—and so our culture learned to develop a more sophisticated methodological skepticism.

As you might guess, I think we're ready for the other shoe to drop. That is, at the moment, we're stuck with only naive belief. Our culture hasn't developed methodological or systematic believing to match methodological doubting. We haven't learned to use belief as a tool—as we use doubt as a tool. That is, over the centuries, we learned to separate the *process of doubting* from the *decision to reject*. But we haven't learned to separate the *process of believing* from the *decision to accept*. This separation that we made in the case of doubting will feel difficult in the case of believing. For the process of believing has caused enormous problems—and still does—while the process of doubting has a good reputation since it became sophisticated: it's born great fruit. Therefore, the process itself of believing feels tainted; our concept of belief tends to connote the decision to accept, that is, to commit. We tend to feel that believing can never be a part of careful thinking.

Since my "Appendix Essay" in *Writing Without Teachers* (1973), I've been trying to describe methodological believing as a discipline—decoupled from commitment, decoupled from naive or temperamental credulity. I've been trying to show that it is possible and that it makes sense to *try* to believe things that we don't believe, especially things we don't want to believe. And that trying can lead to a kind of conditional or temporary believing. People do it all the time, for instance when they hear and read fictional stories—and tell and write them. Just as you don't have to be a skeptical person to use methodological doubting, you don't have to be credulous or weak-minded to believe things temporarily—and try to believe even more.

If this sounds crazy, it's probably because you've forgotten how hard it was to learn methodological doubting. When we were children, it seemed crazy for teachers to tell us that we should doubt ideas that we love. How can I doubt what seems right and precious to me—or doubt someone I trust? How can I doubt that the sun comes up in the morning? (When I taught at MIT, I regularly asked freshman to give me evidence for why the earth spun on its axis and revolved around the sun. Many could not; their basis for accepting this idea was belief in doctrine or authority, not doubt of what's obvious.)

If you still think (naively) that it's easy to practice systematic skepticism—to try to doubt what you want to believe—you need only notice that lots of very smart people still can't do it. We see lots of our colleagues with Ph.D.s who can only doubt ideas they don't like. We give our schools the job of teaching this ability: Whenever people make lists of goals or outcomes for education at every level, *critical thinking* is usually central, and in this case the term usually connotes rational skepticism. Critical thinking, or careful doubting, doesn't come naturally to humans, especially to children. The point of a tool is to learn to do something that doesn't come naturally.

What especially interests me in true methodological doubting is the dimension of *will* or even *emotion*: not just the need for an act of intellect, but also an act of effort or will. No one can make me doubt something I want to believe (for example, the efficacy of freewriting). It won't happen unless I actually try. The good news is that we've built a culture of critical thinking—at least in the academy—that makes me feel that I'm not thinking carefully unless I do try to doubt what I want to believe—even freewriting. This is good. My argument here is that we need to build a richer culture of rationality, richer than mere doubting or critical thinking, so that people will feel that they are not thinking carefully unless they try to believe ideas they don't want to believe.

So just as methodological doubting is not natural, so too methodological believing is not natural. It's not natural to try to believe ideas we disagree with or even hate. It has to be a tool or game that is decoupled from temperament or commitment. In short, methodological doubting and believing are symmetrical and I'm claiming that we need both. In addition to discovering which ideas look best after the scrutiny of doubt, we can discover which ideas look best after the scrutiny of believing. And (as I'll show soon) neither tool can demonstrate that anything is actually true.

THREE ARGUMENTS FOR THE BELIEVING GAME

1. We need the believing game to help us find flaws in our own thinking.

The doubting game is supposed to do this job, of course: not just find other people's bad thinking but find weaknesses in our own thinking. But the doubting game or critical skepticism often falls down on this job.

The flaws in our own thinking usually come from our *assumptions*—our ways of thinking that we accept without noticing—assumptions that are part of the very structure of our thinking. Some assumptions are particularly invisible to us because we are living as part of a community and culture. It's hard to doubt what we live inside of; we can't see it and we unconsciously take it for granted.

Here's where the believing game comes to the rescue. Our best hope for finding invisible flaws in what we can't see in our own thinking is to enter into different ways of thinking or points of view—points of view that carry different assumptions. Only from a new vantage point can we see our normal point of view from the outside and thereby notice problematic assumptions that our customary point of view keeps hidden.

Of course, the doubting game has one method for helping us find flaws in our own assumptions: debate. If we talk with others who disagree with us, and if we accept the rule of the doubting game that all ideas are fair game for debate—even our own cherished ideas—then we have a good chance of finding flaws in what we take for granted.

But most of the people we debate with live inside our culture, even inside our smaller community, and so we often fail to run into people who question these culturally shared assumptions. And even if we do, critical thinking often helps us fend off any criticisms of our ideas or ways of seeing. We see this problem in much academic and intellectual interchange. When smart people are trained only in the tradition of the doubting game, they get better and better at criticizing the ideas they don't like. They use this skill particularly well when they feel a threat to their own ideas or unexamined assumptions.

Yet they feel *justified* in fending off what they don't like because they feel they are engaged in critical thinking. They take refuge in the feeling that they would be "unintellectual" if they said to an opponent what in fact they ought to say: "Your idea sounds really wrong to me. It must be alien to how I think. Let me try to enter into it and get a better perspective on my thinking—and see if there's something important that you can see that I can't see." In short, if we want to be good at finding flaws in our own thinking (a goal that doubters constantly trumpet), we need the believing game.

2. We need the believing game to help us choose among competing positions.

Again, the doubting game is supposed to do this job. But consider some of the typical arguments that swirl around us. Should we invade countries where atrocities are happening? Should we test schoolchildren with nationwide tests in order to improve schools that leave children behind? Should we use grades in teaching?

The doubting game can reveal flaws or bad logic in *arguments* that support one position or another other. But flaws in an argument do not demolish the position itself that these arguments are trying to support. We see this problem everywhere. Over and over we see illogical arguments for good ideas and logical arguments for bad ideas. We can never show that an idea or opinion or position is wrong, only that a supporting argument is wrong. No wonder people so seldom change their minds when someone finds bad reasoning in their argument.

For example, there are arguments for and against military intervention to stop atrocities and for and against national testing and grading. It is possible to find flaws in many of those arguments, but logic cannot show that intervention or national testing or grading are right or wrong. To decide whether to invade or test or grade—these are *decisions* that involve acts of judgment. Decisions or acts of judgment always depend on how much weight to give various arguments. In short—and scientists are often more explicitly aware of this—the doubting game can find flaws, but it can't make decisions for us.

In fact, historians of science have shown cases where scientists have refused to give up on hypotheses that seemed to be disproven by experiments. They say things like "Well, the testing was flawed" and even "This hypothesis is just too beautiful to give up." In effect, they're saying, "The argument for my hypothesis is flawed, but that doesn't mean my hypothesis is wrong." They are making an act of judgment. I'd suggest that when they take positions like these (succumbing, it might be said, to "mere feeling" or "gut thinking"), they are actually using the believing game and finding virtues in a position that the doubting game seems to disqualify. Perhaps the disconfirmation *was* flawed; or perhaps there were flaws in how the position was formulated. But they are not rejecting skeptical testing; they are asking for more time to see if their favored hypothesis might do better in future skeptical testing.

And suppose you are trying to get others to choose among options, that is, you are trying to persuade people who disagree with you. You will probably use the doubting game to show flaws in their arguments. Fair enough. But often (surprise!) they don't change their mind and immediately agree with you. That's because you haven't disproved their position, only their supporting arguments. They won't change their position unless you can get them to see the issue the way you see it. For that, you need the believing game. Of course, you can't force them to take the risk of playing the game—of actually *trying* to believe your position, even hypothetically and temporarily. But the believing game is inherently collaborative. Your have no leverage for asking them to try to believe *your* position unless you start by taking the risk yourself of trying to believe *their* position. The best way to introduce the believing game is to play it and show that you've given a good-faith effort to believe what they believe, even asking them to help you.

The believing game may seem permissive, but there's also a surprising principle of rigor that Wayne Booth (1979) articulated: that we cannot validly *reject* an idea till we've succeeded in dwelling in it—in effect, believing it. If you in your mind dismiss their idea as crazy, or even if you can restate their idea "nicely" but from your alien point of view (the Carl Rogers task), there may be something valuable and correct in it, but you're still too blind to see it. They may seem wrong or crazy—they may *be* wrong or crazy—but nevertheless they may be seeing something that none of us can see.

We may feel totally for or against invading to stop atrocities or national testing or grading, but usually there are gray areas that the believing game is particularly good at uncovering. It might help you believe that there are certain conditions or certain senses in which it makes sense to invade, test, or grade. Most "real-world" practical problems or disputes are deeply hermeneutic—more like interpreting a text than getting the right answer in geometry. To show that a text truly means X does not displace the claim that it also means something quite contrary to X (even if only partly or in certain senses).

Bottom line: The doubting game is a tool. It won't make a decision for us; it just puts us in a better position to exercise judgment about matters that cannot be proven. The believing game is also a tool. Our judging will be more trustworthy if we can use the believing game to find hidden virtues that might exist in positions that are supported by faulty arguments. Tools help us think better. This leads to my third argument for the believing game. It's about thinking.

3. We need the believing game in order to achieve goals that the doubting game neglects.

I've given two arguments for how the believing game helps the doubting game meet its *own* goal. Now I'll argue how the believing game also serves a completely different goal: It develops a different kind of careful thinking from what the doubting game develops—a different dimension of our intelligence or rationality, and also a different way of interacting with others.

This is no argument against the doubting game in itself, since it obviously develops an indispensable dimension of intelligence or rationality. The only thing I'm arguing against is the monopoly of the doubting game in our culture's notion of rationality or careful thinking—a monopoly that has led us to neglect a different and equally indispensable kind of careful thinking.

DOUBTING AND BELIEVING AS WAYS OF USING THE MIND AND FUNCTIONING WITH OTHERS

Phenomenologically, the doubting game teaches us to fend off, spit out, guard ourselves. The believing game teaches us to welcome or swallow. For us sophisticated children of the doubting game, this is not easy: trying to believe an alien idea can make us fear being changed or polluted.

With regard to learning, the doubting game teaches us to extricate or detach ourselves from ideas. In contrast, the believing game teaches us to enter into ideas, to invest or insert ourselves. Wayne Booth (1979) talks about the need to learn to "dwell in" an idea if we want to understand it. Polanyi (1958) insists that there is a "fiduciary transaction"—a core of trust—that is tacit in all learning. As children of the doubting game, we carefully invite our students to read and listen with a skeptical mind, but nevertheless that skepticism will not be very intellectually productive unless students have first fully understood what we want them to view skeptically. This means listening and entering into the words.

Language vs. experience. The doubting game is the rhetoric of *propositions* while the believing game is the rhetoric of *experience.* The doubting game teaches us that we can test or scrutinize points of view better if we put them into propositional form. This helps us bring logic to bear and see hidden contradictions (symbolic logic being the ideal form for scrutinizing thinking). The believing game teaches us to try to understand points of view from the inside. Words can help, but the kind of words that most help us experience ideas tend to be imaginative, metaphorical, narrative, personal, and even poetic words.

But not *just* words. Images and sounds and body movements are particularly helpful for entering into alien ideas. Role-playing—and yes, silence. When someone says something that seems all wrong, the most productive response is often merely to listen and try to digest and not reply at all. Teachers can productively insist on short periods of silence after a controversial point has been made. Not all cultures are so wedded to argument with its proliferation of words. In many cultures silence is felt to correlate with good thinking.

With regard to action. The doubting game teaches us the value of disengaging from action—pausing, standing back, standing on the sidelines. This helps us see flaws we miss when we jump in and act on a point of view. The believing game teaches us to engage or act on an idea—and sometimes we cannot understand something until we've engaged and acted. This is where role playing gets its power: understanding through doing and inhabiting, not debating.

Gender. The doubting game promotes ways of using the mind and being with others that have been associated in our culture with masculinity: arguing, resisting, saying no, pushing away, competing, being aggressive. The believing game promotes mental and social activity that has been associated in our culture with femininity: being compliant, listening, absorbing, swallowing, accepting, saying yes, not arguing back, not sticking up for one's own view. When women play the doubting game—arguing, disagreeing, and debating—they are often seen as less feminine. When men play the believing game—not arguing back, accepting, trying to help the other person's point of view—they are often seen as less masculine.

The individual and social dimensions. The doubting game promotes *both* individualism and social interaction. It promotes individualism by inviting the lone person to question and doubt the group and see the self as separate and different. As Socrates pointed out, logic allows the individual to outvote the group. But the doubting game is also highly social, since it invites us to use others in argument and debate in order to find flaws in what looks reasonable or natural, and especially to find flaws in our own views.

So, too, the doubting game promotes both social action and individualism. It invites the social process of enlisting others to help us look for virtues in what seems hopelessly wrong to us. "Help me see what you see; I can't see it." The believing game doesn't strike me as highly individualistic except in one crucial way: It invites the individual to listen and take seriously her own experience and point of view—even if it looks crazy—and not feel that she must subordinate her perceptions or experience or thinking to that of the group. But it supports this kind of individualism by asking for a flexible, constantly shifting methodological groupishness. It invites an individual who looks crazy to others to say, "Stop arguing with me; just listen for a while. If you can, help me make my position clearer and better."

The Individual and Social Dimensions

Academic life uses the believing game in its central activities: reading, discussion, and writing.

Reading. The believing game helps us enter more fully into texts that we find difficult or alien—and also helps us discover and understand a wider range of interpretations. We want to teach students critical thinking, but they also need to learn to enter into texts that feel alien to them, to dwell in them and experience them, not stay untouched and outside them.

Discussion. Because of the dominance of critical thinking, especially in the academy, academics and students tend to feel that the best way to show they are smart is by pointing out flaws in the views of others. Discussions can take an adversarial tone. People tend to feel "un-smart" when they don't see the flaws that "smart" people point out—or when they say something like "What? Tell me more about that. I'm trying to see it as you see it." Discussions tend to be more fruitful if we have more people giving this believing game response. (In discussions among philosophers, it often counts as an indictment when someone says, "I fail to be able to understand your train of thought." This response shows the monopoly of the doubting game in academic culture and the fear of trying to believe ideas you don't like.)

Writing. Our current model for academic or essayist writing tends to be adversarial. When people write an essay advancing a position, especially in the academy, they are usually expected start off trying to show that all other points of view are wrong. This ritual is wrong epistemologically: views that seem contrary can both be true—and even if "they" are wrong, that doesn't make you right. And it's wrong rhetorically: you are asking your reader to admit defeat as a precondition to listening to your ideas. The believing game suggests modes of writing persuasively and analytically that are nonadversarial.

CONCLUDING REFLECTIONS

The believing game is alive in our midst—but not well. Look more closely at people who are deeply smart and creative rather than just quick in debate; people who work out new ideas and creative solutions rather than just criticizing what others believe or propose; people who collaborate productively with others and bring about action. I think you'll see that the believing game underlies much of the good work these people do.

But because of our current model of good thinking (rational skepticism or the doubting game), most of us lack the lens or the language to see the skill these people exhibit as intellectual sophistication or careful thinking—the skill of genuinely dwelling in ideas different from their own. When we see them listening and drawing out others, we call them generous or nice rather than smart. We don't connect good listening to intelligence. We say, "Isn't it wonderful how they can mobilize others and actually get things done," but we see that as a social and personal gift rather than an intellectual skill. We call creativity a mystery. And because our intellectual model is flawed in these ways, we don't teach this ability to enter into alien ideas.

A parting testament to the doubting game. In case you think I'm biased against the doubting game, let me acknowledge that this whole chapter is an exercise in skeptical doubting. I am using the doubting game as a tool to try to undermine what I see as a monopoly of the doubting game. I'm not trying to get rid of the doubting game—merely to add the believing game.

FINAL REFLECTION

The doubting game and the believing game are tools or methods. As such, they cannot make decisions for us. Consider the claim, "I can improve the world by teaching." The doubting game can't prove that it's wrong; the believing game can't prove that it's right. To go on with our lives, it's a question of whether to trust a view or stance. And that's a matter of judgment, not proof. But our judgments will be better if we get to use both tools.

In burned-out moments it's easy and natural to doubt that we can improve the world by teaching. But what if we put genuine effort into actually believing it? I'm not arguing that it will lead to full belief, but that it will lead us to see and understand things unavailable to us from a position of skepticism and detachment. For many teachers, the process of trying to believe their early "naive" view involves having to undergo feelings of sadness, pain, even loss, but also seeing more clearly a path toward fulfillment instead of bitterness. In the end, I'm arguing for a richer and more accurate picture of rationality or intelligence or careful thinking.

REFERENCES

Booth, W. (1979). *Critical understanding: The powers and limits of pluralism.* Chicago: University of Chicago Press.

Booth, W. (2005, March). Blind skepticism versus a rhetoric of assent. *College English, 67*(4), 377–388.

Elbow, P. (1973). Appendix essay: The doubting game and the believing game: An analysis of the intellectual process. In *Writing without teachers* (pp. 147–191). Oxford: Oxford University Press.

Elbow, P. (1982, Winter). The doubting game and the believing game. *Pre/Text: An Inter-Disciplinary Journal of Rhetoric, 3*(4).

Elbow, P. (1986). Methodological doubting and believing: Contraries in inquiry. In *Embracing Contraries: Explorations in learning and teaching* (pp. 254–300). Oxford: Oxford University Press.

Elbow, P. (2000). The believing game: A challenge after twenty-five years. In *Everyone can write: Essays toward a hopeful theory of writing and teaching writing* (pp. 76–80.). New York: Oxford University Press.

Elbow, P. (2005, March). Bringing the rhetoric of assent and the believing game together—and into the classroom. *College English, 67*(4), 388–399.

Elbow, P. (2006). The believing game and how to make conflicting opinions more fruitful." In C. Weber (Ed.), *Nurturing the peacemakers in our students: A guide to teaching peace, empathy, and understanding* (pp. 16–25). Portsmouth, NH: Heinemann.

Elbow, P. (2009, Winter). The believing game or methodological believing. *Journal for the Assembly for Expanded Perspectives on Learning, 14,* 1–11.

Polanyi, M. (1958). *Personal knowledge: Toward a post-critical philosophy.* New York: Harper & Row.

Chapter 11

Five Alive:
Why Teaching Is So Compelling

Patricia A. Wasley

L AST YEAR I TAUGHT A CLASS AGAIN after not teaching for several years. Given that I began teaching nearly 35 years ago, I was surprised to feel all of the emotional charges that one gets from teaching: the nervousness, the sleepless night before the first class, the excitement, the OMG-will-I-be-a-dud fears, and the constant running checklist review: syllabus, check; readings, check; videos, check; discussion prompts, check. There is the "please-let-the-technology-actually-work" prayer. And my reccurring dream: I can't wake up; my feet will not move quickly; I cannot seem to get out the door, and I am late, so late, for my class.

The reason teaching is so compelling, I think, is because it requires the "teacher" to move into the learning mode, not just about the subject matter but about the *students,* and all the emotions and psychological issues listed above kick into gear again. Teaching makes me feel more alive *because* I begin learning again, and it is not the learning of routine—the dusting off of old lesson plans, the shaking out of a talk I have given before—but the learning that one must do when one is starting anew, starting fresh.

The feelings and senses embedded in learning something new are central to what makes teaching so compelling. I am one of those people who absolutely love to travel. In the United States or out—doesn't matter. The issue is going somewhere new. The reason I love it is because when I set out on my first day in a new place, everything is unfamiliar and fresh. It's almost as if my vision clears because I am seeing things for the first time. My nose picks up the differences in the way the streets, the coffee, the restaurants, the countryside smells. My ears hear things with greater acuity: new kinds of ambulance sirens, new horns honking, different bird song. The texture of new places is different, so I find myself wanting to touch everything. All the senses are at work, and that feeling of fresh aliveness elevates me spiritually, emotionally, physically. I just plain feel, well, more *alive*.

The act of teaching is similar: The class files in. My eyesight clears and sharpens as I study the new faces of my students, the way they walk, the shape of their backpacks, in order to learn anything that might help me unlock the system of learning for that particular student. I catch the scent of the art room—someone really likes to paint. Or I get a whiff of cigarette smoke or perfume or hairspray—each a clue to these new people. I see iPods and if I can glimpse what's playing, I hear in my mind's ear a bit of their chosen rhythm, their musical home space. I watch kids text, thumbs flying, eyes on the screen, and know they have friends and/or family with whom they are communicating, just like I do. All my senses are attuned to learn about the learners. And, frankly, all those senses are necessary!

The act of teaching is like going to a murder mystery dinner or reading a mystery. From the very beginning, there is a sure sense that things we haven't anticipated will arise. Slowly but surely clues begin to assemble themselves, like puzzle pieces with big gaps between the edges and the middle. The tension builds as the clues build. As a reader/dinner guest, I arrange, then rearrange the clues, trying to figure out who did it, and I feel a sense of urgency. It is important that I figure this out before something more drastic happens!

In my classroom each student I encounter is different and when they walk into the room for the very first time, I feel a sense of dramatic tension rising: Which ones will love what I have planned for us? Which of them will find it excruciatingly boring? Which of them has the skills they need to be successful? Who has had teachers and/or family members tell them they aren't good at reading or thinking or writing or speaking? For which of them will this be the last chance they might have to learn the skills and abilities I wish to convey? I feel a sense of real tension rising, building.

Each hears what I say in a different way. If I say to my class that the streets of New York City are so crowded they feel like bumper cars, someone from Ferndale, Washington, pictures bumper cars at the county fair—six little cars going around in a wide circle—or the traffic light in town where things get jammed up. Their mental picture, based on what they know, is quite different from what it is *really* like walking down Fifth Avenue anytime during the Thanksgiving weekend, where you can't help but bump into other people, or walking through any subway station at rush hour, where, again, you are constantly dodging and jostling others. So I always have to think: What has their life experience been like? How are they picturing and thinking about what I want them to learn?

The important thing to remember while teaching is that the teacher has as many mysteries to solve as there are students in the room. Each student relates the new material to his own past experience, and that is what makes teaching so difficult, so challenging, and so very interesting. Teachers have to use all their senses, to be awake and alert to learning about their students in order to help their students unlock their own learning. Teaching requires incredible attention to detail, to clues. It requires excellent observational skills, a good sense of smell, hearing, seeing, listening, tasting. Teaching is so very much more than simply delivering information; it is about unlocking human potential. To do that well, the teacher has to have all five senses awake and alive, fresh and at the ready to help other human beings learn what they need to successfully negotiate our world. It is fun, it is investigative, it is heartbreaking at times, and it is always important. As I sit planning my classes for next year, I feel lucky to have work that requires that I shake myself fully present, that I dust off each sensory system and give a fresh drop of oil to my learning tools. Teaching requires that *I* come to the table prepared to learn in order to fulfill the role of a teacher.

Chapter 12

Holding the Tension of Opposites

PARKER PALMER

HOLDING THE TENSION OF PARADOX so that our students can learn at deeper levels is among the most difficult demands of good teaching. How are we supposed to do it?

Imagine yourself in a classroom. You ask a well-framed question, and then you wait and wait as the great silence descends. You know you should wait some more, not jump, but your heart pounds, then sinks, and finally feels helpless and out of control. So you answer your own question with an emotional mix of anxiety, anger, and authoritarianism that only makes things worse. Then you watch as the opening to learning offered by the silence vanishes—and teaching becomes more and more like running headlong into walls.

That scenario—which could apply to holding any of the paradoxes, not just silence and speech—suggests a simple truth: the place where paradoxes are held together is in the teacher's heart, and our inability to hold them is less a failure of technique than a gap in our inner lives. If we want to teach and learn in the power of paradox, we must rededicate our hearts.

In particular, we must teach our hearts a new way to understand the tension we feel when we are torn between the poles. Some clues to such an understanding are found in E. F. Schumacher's classic text, *Small Is Beautiful* (1975):

Through all our lives we are faced with the task of reconciling opposites which, in logical thought, cannot be reconciled. . . . How can one reconcile the demands of freedom and discipline in education? Countless mothers and teachers, in fact, do it, but no one can write down a solution. They do it by bringing into the situation a force that belongs to a higher level where opposites are transcended—the power of love. . . . Divergent problems, as it were, force us to strain ourselves to a level above ourselves; they demand, and thus provoke the supply of, forces from a higher level, thus bringing love, beauty, goodness and truth into our lives. It is only with the help of these higher forces that the opposites can be reconciled in the living situation. (pp. 79–80)

Schumacher's words help me understand that the tension that comes when I try to hold a paradox together is not hell-bent on tearing me apart. Instead, it is a power that wants to pull my heart open to something larger than myself. The tension always feels difficult, sometimes destructive. But if I can collaborate with the work it is trying to do rather than resist it, the tension will not break my heart—it will make my heart larger.

Schumacher's illustration of this point is brilliant because it is true to ordinary experience: Every good teacher and every good parent has somehow learned to negotiate the paradox of freedom and discipline. We want our children and our students to become people who think and live freely, yet at the same time we know that helping them become free requires us to restrict their freedom in certain situations.

Of course, neither our children nor our students share this knowledge! When my 13-year-old son announces that he will no longer attend religious services or a student submits a paper on a topic other than the one I assigned, I am immediately drawn into the tension—and there is no formula to tell me whether this is a moment for freedom or discipline or some alchemy of both.

But good teachers and good parents find their way through such minefields every day by allowing the tension itself to pull them open to a larger and larger love—a love that resolves these Solomonic dilemmas by looking past the tension within ourselves toward the best interests of the student or the child.

As always with profound truths, there is a paradox about this love. Schumacher says that a good parent or teacher resolves the tension of divergent problems by embodying the transcendent power of love. Yet he also says that resolving the tension requires a supply of love that comes from beyond ourselves, provoked by the tension itself. If we are to hold paradoxes together, our own love is absolutely necessary—and yet our own love is never enough. In a time of tension, we must endure with whatever love we can muster until that tension draws a larger love into the scene.

There is a name for the endurance we must practice until a larger love arrives: It is called suffering. We will not be able to teach in the power of paradox until we are willing to suffer the tension of opposites, until we understand that such suffering is neither to be avoided nor merely to be survived but must be actively embraced for the way it expands our own hearts.

Without this acceptance, the pain of suffering will always lead us to resolve the tension prematurely, because we have no reason to stand the gaff. We will ask and answer our own questions in the silence of the classroom (thus creating more silence); we will ride roughshod over the dissenting voice that confounds our learning plan (even though we said we welcomed questions); we will punish the student who writes outside the assignment (no matter how creatively) to bring her back in line.

We cannot teach our students at the deepest levels when we are unable to bear the suffering that opens into those levels. By holding the tension of opposites, we hold the gateway to inquiry open, inviting students into a territory in which we all can learn.

How to do this is not a question that can be answered, for it is done in the teacher's heart: Holding the tension of opposites is about being, not doing. But some words from Rilke may help. They offer no technique for embracing suffering, because one does not exist. But they offer hope for what might happen if we tried.

The words are from *Letters to a Young Poet*, in which Rilke (1962) writes as a teacher. He had received a series of respectful but demanding letters from a neophyte who admired Rilke's work and sought advice on how to follow in his path. Rilke not only took the time to respond but did so with astonishing generosity.

In one exchange, the young poet presses the older one with question after urgent question, and Rilke replies with this counsel:

> Be patient toward all that is unsolved in your heart and try to love the questions themselves. . . . . Do not now seek the answers, which cannot be given you because you would not be able to live them. And the point is, to live everything. Live the questions now. Perhaps you will then gradually, without noticing it, live along some distant day into the answer. (p. 35).

His words could easily be paraphrased to speak to the condition of the teacher whose heart is unable to hold the tension of opposites in the classroom: Be patient toward all that is unresolved in your heart. . . . Try to love the contradictions themselves. . . . Do not now seek the resolutions, which cannot be given you because you would not be ready to live them—and the point is to live everything. Live the contradictions now. Perhaps you will then gradually, without noticing it, live along some distant day into the paradox.

The hope Rilke gives me lies partly in his notion that on "some distant day" I might find that I have lived my way into a more confident understanding of how to hold the tension of paradox than I have at this moment. Surely he is right about that: Having lived into the tensions of teaching for some time now, I am better able to hold paradoxes together than I was years ago.

But my deeper hope comes with Rilke's words "and the point is to live everything." Of course that is the point! If I do not fully live the tensions that come my way, those tensions do not disappear: they go underground and multiply. I may not know how to solve them, but by wrapping my life around them and trying to live out their resolution, I open myself to new possibilities and keep the tensions from tearing me apart.

There is only one alternative: an unlived life, a life lived in denial of the tensions that teaching brings. Here, I play a masked professional role, pretending outwardly that I have no tensions at all while inwardly all those tensions I pretend not to have are ripping the fabric of my life.

Pretending is another name for dividedness, a state that keeps us from cultivating the capacity for connectedness on which good teaching depends. When we pretend, we fall out of community with ourselves, our students, and the world around us, out of communion with the common center that is both the root and the fruit of teaching at its best. But when we understand that "the point is to live everything," we will recover all that is lost.

I give the last word on this subject to Florida Scott-Maxwell (1975), who, writing toward the end of a long and well-lived life, speaks with authority:

> Some uncomprehended law holds us at a point of contradiction where we have no choice, where we do not live that which we love, where good and bad are inseparable partners impossible to tell apart, and where we—heart-broken and ecstatic—can only resolve the conflict by blindly taking it into our hearts. This used to be called being in the hands of God. Has anyone any better words to describe it? (pp. 86–90).

REFERENCES

Rilke, R. M. (1962). *Letters to a young poet*. New York: W.W. Norton.

Schumacher, E. F. (1974). *Small is beautiful: Economics as if people mattered*. New York: HarperCollins.

Scott-Maxwell, F. (1975). *The measure of my days: The private notebook of a remarkable woman of eighty-two*. New York: Knopf.

Chapter 13

The High School Teacher as Scholar?

SAM SCHEER

NOW THAT I HAVE BEEN TEACHING ENGLISH for almost 30 years, my colleagues—both old and young—keep asking me when I am going to retire. "Never," I taunt them. "It took me a lifetime to learn how to teach. Why would I stop now?" Given the fact that many of the older veterans in my large and diverse high school wordlessly greet each other by holding up one, two, or three fingers to indicate the years of servitude they must endure before they get their pension, I am not surprised by their incredulity; but it is heartbreaking that so many of my young colleagues find it unfathomable that anyone would stay in the classroom for 5 years, let alone beyond the time when would one could retire with full benefits. To be fair, the working conditions in my school are difficult. Large classes, behavior problems, and a curriculum often driven by high-stakes testing are discouraging and can test the resolve of even the most committed teachers. But for me at least, the joy of being able to earn a living by studying literature and sharing my studies with young people trumps all the difficulties.

Proposing study as an antidote to teacher frustration as well as an effective Rx for teacher burnout is not likely to win many converts. Indeed, when I proposed this theory to a colleague, she told me bluntly, "The kids don't need a scholar, they need a collar!" and "Hey, how much do you have to know to be a high school teacher?" If a lifetime of teaching has taught me anything, it is the certainty that the only responsible answer to my colleague's question is, "More than one can ever know." Arguing for the teacher's need of abundant knowledge, John Dewey (1986) makes the same point and then some in his book *How We Think*:

> The practically important question concerns the conditions under which the teacher can really be the intellectual leader of a social group. The first condition goes back to his intellectual preparation in subject matter. This should be abundant to the point of overflow. It must be much wider than the ground laid out in textbook or in any fixed plan for teaching a lesson. It must cover collateral points, so that the teacher can take advantage of unexpected questions or unanticipated incidents. It must be accompanied by a genuine enthusiasm for the subject that will communicate itself contagiously to pupils. (p. 338)

The "intellectual preparation" that Dewey ascribes to teacher effectiveness has always been for me a source of great pleasure. The joy that comes from study is profound and in teaching, that joy is even more profound because one's own progress is so inextricably joined to the progress of the students who are in one's charge. Reading Samuel Johnson on Milton or Helen Vendler on Elizabeth Bishop may not, for example, be of immediate use in my classroom, but by stretching and exercising my mind, these great scholars and others make me a bit more supple and ready to field my students' questions when they do arise. Here again, Dewey (1986) seems to have it just right:

> The teacher must have his mind free to observe the mental responses and movements of the student members of the recitation group. The problem of the pupils is found in subject matter; the problem of teachers is what the minds of pupils are doing with the subject matter. Unless the teacher's mind has mastered the subject in advance, unless it is thoroughly at home in it, using it unconsciously without the need of express thought, he will not be free to give full time and attention to observations and interpretation of the pupils' intellectual reactions. (p. 338)

Teaching is a kind of deep play, and if one is going to make that play pleasurable and meaningful for students, teachers must learn the history and rules of the game that govern the discipline they teach. Given the fractured syntax, the half-formed utterances, and puzzled exhalations that often characterize my students' first response to new works, the only way to get them in the game is to be able to pitch the text at a dozen speeds and angles until each and every one of them can make contact. Such mastery takes much study and practice, but the crack of the bat sounds sweet. After many long years of hard work, my classroom has begun to feel more like a kind of intellectual baseball field than the pedagogical factory it did when I first began teaching. On good days—and there are many of them—I can choose, as required by circumstance, to be the coach, umpire, pinch hitter, centerfielder, cleanup batter, or just an appreciative fan watching a young player with endless potential. To give up such a life before I must seems the height of ingratitude, especially when so many people are condemned to work at jobs they hate.

If you believe, as I do, that teaching—no less than art—demands one's deepest commitment, then study and preparation take on something of a spiritual dimension. Part of what keeps me fresh is not only formal literary study, but also reflecting on the craft and best practice of the teachers I have encountered at various stages of my life. My greatest teacher was Andy Galligani, whose colleagues affectionately called him the Socrates of the Pine Barrens. Impoverished and crippled with polio as a child, he grew up on a dusty farm and subsisted on nothing but potatoes and poetry. Rescued by his intellect and a high school teacher who encouraged him to apply for a university scholarship, he made his way to Rutgers University and from there to a public high school in central New Jersey. No Old Testament prophet could have had a more profound influence on me. Galligani had seemingly memorized half the poems in the English language and he insisted that his students memorize a poem each week. A poem, he told our class filled with farmers' sons and daughters, is better than a birthday. Reciting Emerson's (1909) essay "The Poet" with a voice that rang down the hallway, Galligani declared:

With what joy I begin to read a poem, which I confide in as an inspiration! And now my chains are to be broken; I shall mount about these clouds and opaque airs in which I live—opaque, though they seem transparent—and from the heaven of truth I shall see and comprehend my relations. That will reconcile me to life, and renovate nature, to see trifles animated by a tendency, and to know what I am doing. Life will no more be a noise; now I shall see men and women, and know the signs by which they may be discerned from fools and satans. This day shall be better than my birthday; then I became an animal: now I am invited into the science of the real. (p. 172)

Many students in the class thought Galligani was nuts, but they still loved him and his passion for his subject. For me, listening to him talk about literature was like hearing the music of the spheres. After I graduated, we became lifelong friends, and much of what I still do in the classroom—including asking my students to memorize poems—comes from the model he provided me. All along the way, Galligani seemed to know what question I needed to frame, even before I could bring it fully to mind. And this knack, above all, is the mark of a great teacher. As far as I know, Galligani did not publish anything except a few fierce letters in the local newspaper. Still, he left dinosaur footprints.

Fortunately, some of the greatest teachers of all time like Plato, Aristotle, Rousseau, and John Dewey have left a published record of their thoughts on teaching, and they too have provided me with models that I can adopt or modify to suit the needs of my students. An hour with these thinkers is worth a week of what passes these days for professional development. Sadly, most of my young colleagues were never introduced to these thinkers as part of their own preparation to be teachers and choose instead to model their teaching on the inane and changing curricular mandates from the state. No wonder they get burned out and want to leave the profession! There have been, to be sure, advances in cognitive science and technology that teachers ignore at their students' peril, but much of what passes for change in education is largely due, as Robert Frost (1914/1991) wrote, to "truths being in and out of favour" (p. 55). Having recently spent time reading the latest teacher training manuals and rereading *The Republic,* I feel confident in casting my vote for Plato.

The sacred task of every teacher is to awaken the consciousness of his or her students and to help them live beyond themselves in possibility. As an English teacher, I want my students to hear the living voices of the great authors we study and to discover in them what Wallace Stevens (1951) calls "the precious portents of our own powers" (pp. 174–175). When I greet my students and begin to teach each day, I want to be for them what my great teachers have been to me: a loyal friend of the mind. To be faithful to my students and to honor the memory of my own intellectual mentors, I must love and study my subject as best as I can. For me, teaching is—or at least it should be—the scholar's art.

REFERENCES

Dewey, J. (1986). *Essays and how we think: Volume 8 of John Dewey's later works, 1925–1953* (J.A. Boydston, Ed.). Carbondale, IL: Southern Illinois University Press.

Eeckhout, B. (2002). *Wallace Stevens and the limits of reading and writing.* Columbia, MO: University of Missouri Press.

Emerson, R. W. (1909). *Essays and English traits: The Harvard classics, vol. 5 (1909–1914) of Ralph Waldo Emerson* (C. W. Eliot, Ed.). New York: P.F. Collier & Son.

Frost, R. (1991). The black cottage. In *Poems by Robert Frost: A boy's will and North of Boston* (pp. 50–55). New York: Signet. (Original work published 1914)

Stevens, W. (1951). *The necessary angel: Essays on reality and the imagination.* New York: Random House.

Chapter 14

The World Becomes What You Teach: A Better World Through Humane Education

ZOE WEIL

I TAUGHT MY FIRST HUMANE EDUCATION COURSES IN 1987. I was in graduate school, looking for a summer job, and I heard about a program at the University of Pennsylvania that offered week-long summer classes to seventh and eighth graders. I called the director of the program and pitched 5 courses. She said yes to all of them. There were 60 courses offered that summer and not nearly enough students to fill them, but 3 of the 5 ran: Creative Writing, Environmental Issues, and Animal Issues (Critical Television Watching and World Religions did not, which in retrospect does not seem too surprising). The course on animals turned out to be the second most popular that summer, a testament to students' interest in learning about a pressing social issue and what they could to stop cruelty and suffering.

I watched in amazement as the students changed over the course of the week; in one case, overnight. I had taught about product testing on animals on Wednesday (in which shampoos, oven cleaners, cosmetics, and other personal care and household products are squeezed into the eyes of conscious rabbits and force-fed to them in quantities that kill), and Thursday morning a boy in the class came in and showed me the leaflets he'd made on the subject the night before. He asked if he could hand them out on the street at lunch. He'd become an activist in 24 hours.

I stayed in touch with a couple of the students from that course. One wrote me a letter that fall about how inspired she was to make a difference. She signed up for the environmental course I taught the next summer and then she and another boy from the original class asked if I would continue to teach them during the school year. They went to different schools so I invited them to come to my house after school where we would learn about more issues. They invited some of their friends and then started a Philadelphia area student activist group, which was active throughout their high school years. This was the beginning of my career as a humane educator, someone who teaches about the interconnected issues of human rights, environmental preservation, and animal protection in an effort to inspire conscientious choice-making and engaged change-making for a humane, peaceful, and sustainable world.

For many years I ran a humane education program for a non-profit organization. I visited schools daily in the greater Philadelphia region offering courses, classroom presentations, after-school programs, assemblies, and teacher professional development that covered a range of humane issues. I observed the effect that even a single presentation could have: raising interest, captivating attention, drawing out critical thinking, and inspiring student clubs and change-making efforts.

I was reaching about 10,000 students a year, which sounds like a lot, but I wanted every student's education to include learning about important issues that were neglected in the traditional curriculum. So in 1996 I cofounded the Institute for Humane Education (IHE) primarily to train people to be humane educators so that there would be thousands of teachers bringing humane education to students across the globe. We launched the first Humane Education Certificate Program and Master of Education program that focused on humane education in the United States. Our goals were to prepare and inspire teachers to be humane educators who bring relevant issues of the day into their existing curricula and to promote humane education so that courses on interconnected global ethical challenges would become ubiquitous.

We based our teacher training on the four elements that comprise quality humane education:

1. Providing accurate information about the challenges of our time so students acquire the knowledge to make informed, conscious choices
2. Fostering the 3 Cs of curiosity, creativity, and critical thinking so students are enthusiastic about and skilled at tackling challenges
3. Instilling the 3 Rs of reverence, respect, and responsibility so students are motivated to work for healthy changes
4. Offering positive choices and the tools for problem-solving so students become conscientious choice-makers and successful change-makers

Then Congress passed the No Child Left Behind Act of 2001 (NCLB), and schools and teachers had to hunker down to teach "the basics." In the early 1990s critical thinking courses were welcomed; a decade later the term was sometimes criticized as "soft" work in a society that now wanted education to focus on competing with China, which largely meant trying to get higher scores on math and science tests.

How was I going to stay "burned in" during these dark times for innovative teachers who believe education is the greatest tool for creating positive change in the world? Because I wasn't a classroom teacher, I didn't have to teach to endless standardized and/or high-stakes tests, but I was educating teachers, and unless I could demonstrate how humane education issues fit into their "learning results" and NCLB standards-based curricula, the teachers who came to us wouldn't find our professional development very practical.

I balked at this need to fit everything into state and national curriculum standards, and I began to see the fundamental purpose of education in the United States as misguided. Obviously, everyone needs to be verbally, mathematically, and scientifically literate, but I began to question our basic assumptions about the educational goals we as a society were striving to achieve.

I came up with this thought experiment: Imagine if all children graduated from high school having passed their NCLB tests year after year with flying colors. Imagine further that every graduate was able to get a job (or go to college and get a job or go to college and graduate school and get a job) so that we had full employment in our nation. Would we feel as a society that we'd succeeded in our goals for education? I think most people would say yes. But would we be satisfied with this? Should this be our ultimate goal? Is it good enough?

In a world confronting such extraordinary challenges as global warming, alarming and growing rates of species extinction, human overpopulation (with one-sixth of our species lacking access to clean water or enough food), escalating worldwide slavery, pollution, and resource depletion, to name a few of our biggest problems, is it enough to graduate students who are simply literate and employable?

I don't think so. I think that our graduates must be skilled "solutionaries" who have the knowledge, tools, and motivation to transform systems that are unsustainable and destructive into ones that are healthy and just. No matter what field our graduates pursue—whether business, farming, health care, politics, education, law, architecture, engineering, and so on—they must be prepared to be change agents who bring creativity, critical thinking, and innovation to their work so that they do the most good and the least harm to all people, animals, and the environment. This, I believe, ought to be the true purpose of education.

Recently, I was the speaker at the National Honors Society induction at our local high school. As part of my talk I asked the audience to analyze a conventional cotton T-shirt and describe the effects, both positive and negative, of this item on themselves, other people, animals, and the environment. In a few minutes, we'd touched upon child slavery in the cotton fields of Asia, pesticide exposure and contamination, sweatshops, toxic dyes, excessive use of fossil fuels, and more. I invited the inductees to perceive themselves as future solutionaries, who in whatever careers they might pursue would use their great minds and big hearts for noble purposes, and who would create new systems that promote prosperity and peace so that the clothing we produce, through every part of its "life cycle," is humane and safe. I then asked them to consider this same imperative in relation to everything we produce, from food to electronics to buildings to forms of transportation. After the talk a friend asked one of the inductees what she thought of my presentation. She replied that it made her angry that she'd never been taught any of these issues before and exclaimed, "We should have been learning this since kindergarten!"

I agree. That's why I became a humane educator.

A few months later I was speaking at an event in New York City in honor of the International Day of Peace. I invited one of the students from my first humane education course (back in 1987) to attend. He's now a 35-year-old man working in public health for Mayor Bloomberg on HIV/AIDS issues. I hadn't seen him in 16 years. After the talk I introduced him as a student in my first humane ed class, and he immediately piped in, "That course changed my life!"

This is why I continue to be a humane educator.

What keeps me committed is the fervent belief that education is the most effective way to create a peaceful, sustainable, and humane world. Were we to decide to embrace this bigger, more important purpose for schooling, I believe that we could change the world dramatically for the better in a single generation by graduating engaged, impassioned, imaginative, skilled young women and men eager to play crucial roles in creating energy, food, construction, waste, economic, legal, political, production, health, and other systems that are safe, just, and restorative.

What keeps me committed, even in these dark days of excessive standardized tests, reduction in art programs, low morale, limited funding, and school violence, is the wave of committed educators and innovative ideas and programs that are infusing even the most unlikely schools with imaginative and dedicated approaches.

What keeps me committed are those students who time and again have let me know that this kind of education, humane education, is life-changing and potentially world-transforming. Although I spend most of my days writing for and training adults, I still go into classrooms periodically. After a weeklong miniblock in humane education for a local eighth-grade class last year, I received a packet of letters. Here are excerpts from just two of them:

Spending that week with you was the most inspiring 5 days of my life so far. You made me realize how much just one person can do to help the world and how much more you can do by educating others about the issues. I have already started teaching my parents. . . . It feels really good to know that I can take sometimes simple and sometimes complex actions to save a life and our world. Thank you so much for this opportunity! I will carry that week with me for a lifetime.

Thank you so much for coming to our class and teaching us about some of the great problems of the world, but most importantly, how we can help. I was really inspired by you, and I really can't wait to get started. . . . I have no doubt that last week will stay with me my entire life, and [I] thank you for giving me that experience and the courage to change the world.

To me, these letters are a testament to the power and promise of humane education. Young people are so thirsty for meaning and purpose, so eager to be of value and use in this world, so enriched by the joy that comes from focusing their intelligence and creativity toward a greater goal. Yet so much of their current schooling fails them, not because they don't have committed teachers, but because the very purpose of schooling fails them. Their teachers are so busy cramming disparate and often seemingly irrelevant information into their saturated minds when what they yearn for is knowledge that helps them be of value, that sparks their curiosity and engages their hands, minds, and hearts in deep and innovative thinking and purposeful and satisfying doing.

Those teachers who spend each day infusing their courses with such meaning, who engage their otherwise bored students, who re-ignite their inborn passion for learning, who hold the bar high for each child based on that child's capacities and watch these same children exceed their expectations, cannot help but stay burned in because the rewards of such achievements are huge. We educators hold the key to a better future, and when we see the potential of that future unfold through the efforts of those students we've taught, encouraged, and helped, we realize there is nothing we could do that better serves our own highest selves and our aspirations for a better world.

Chapter 15

What, You Wanted An Easy Problem?

KIRSTEN OLSON

We go to school to learn to be stupid.

—Ivan Illich, *Deschooling Society*

A RECENT *NEW YORK TIMES* ARTICLE (Rich, 2009), profiling a middle school teacher in Georgia who reorganized her English classes to allow children to choose their own books, was one of the most furor-inducing educational pieces the *Times* has recently published. Some months after its appearance, people are still getting online to rail and object to the outrageous notion that allowing middle school children to choose the novels they read, based on their own lives and prior reading experiences, is more likely to engage them in class and to support them to become lifelong readers. (In the case of the teacher profiled, her methods also produced higher test scores.) The article carefully describes how the teacher "nudged" her students to choose more and more challenging reading selections throughout the year (and they did), but the teacher also had to put up with a lot of administrative flack and pushback from her colleagues, who didn't want to give up their textbooks or class novels. Ultimately, confirmed in her methods, the teacher won the support of her principal, if not her sister and brother teachers. Students' reading habits, the teacher said, were transformed. But the comments from *New York Times'* readers were mostly negative, about how much students will mess around and not learn "discipline" if this teacher keeps on instructing this way.

One of the most confounding issues that every young teacher will confront, if he or she is alive and awake, is that many conventional school settings really aren't about learning at all. They are designed to "teach" children other things: compliance in a hierarchical system, acceptance of values and ideas that may not be their own, and a sense that someone else, not them, is in charge of what is important in learning—that one's own preferences hardly matter. ("We have to prepare them for the *real* world," as many administrators and teachers say.) Even in privileged academic environments there is round-the-clock grinding that teaches students that success is about mind-numbing endurance and the ability to tolerate academic hazing without complaint. (Enjoy it. It's good for you!)

Why then, become a teacher? What draws millions of promising young people to this work?

Most newly budded teachers come to the work with hearts pumped plump with idealism. I know this because my undergraduate education students write essays about this every year, and in these essays I recognize myself. They and I imagine ourselves before a group of adoring children or young adults, in the act of setting kids afire with a love of learning. For the first time in their school lives, they will be free to go where their own passions take them! In this fantasy, preschoolers or second graders or even moody, sassy, troubled high schoolers are afire with humor and vitality to learn, all gathered in, the former rules and boundaries of learning and dumb teacher talk transgressed! These pupils adore us because we are *sooo different from every stupid teacher we ever had.*

OK, just try it. In my first year of teaching, at a fine undergraduate college, I tried to instruct without many rules. "I'm your friend," I suggested to my students. "I'm on your side. We're going to put this course together mutually." I had just gotten out of graduate school, and the tyranny of White male professordom. "I understand. Really. I want us to do something different!" My students were sullen, blank, and cross. Hey, I thought this course was an easy A in the education department! I just want to come in, listen to the lecture (not really), write the three papers, take the exams, and get out. Please don't complicate this. Also, you, teacher, don't have the reputation yet to get us all excited about doing so much work for you. You haven't got the institutional cojones to pull this off! What are you trying to do anyway? How can we trust you when we don't know anything about you?

The next year I tried, against my principles, to be more "traditional." I didn't ask students to grade themselves, keep a portfolio of their work, or write endless self-reflective essays. I hired teaching assistants to run discussion groups and handed out rubrics for written work I'd gotten off the Internet. Another misjudgment. Although the students understood the rules perfectly, I hated teaching this way. My heart just wasn't in it. My teaching assistants, sensing that they might need to become the harsh end of institutional law, became whip-toting dominatrixes of the grade book: jamming kids (their peers) for handing papers in late, grading without much sense of heart or meaning, taking attendance vociferously, not accepting work that wasn't in the right format. They became enforcers. (I say this like I knew what was going on, but I really didn't. This is all with the benefit of hindsight.)

So finally, like Goldilocks, in the third year I started to get it just right. I spent a lot of time carefully explaining where I was coming from as a teacher. I didn't have any teaching assistants, which put my face first in every student-teacher interaction. (This was much more work, of course.) By the third year at this institution students did know me better, and they were more willing to come along with me on an educational journey, to grade themselves, to reflect openly about what had happened to them in educational institutions in the past, to "own" the class as a space where they might actually say something powerful, important, and new about themselves.

But whew, did I need a break from teaching after my third year! I was so exhausted! Portfolios scattered across my entire house for months, my endless comments about the thoughtfulness of the work became almost a point of satire to myself. (*Thoughtful* became my favorite word, and their work really was thoughtful, but I was getting sick of myself.) My husband unhappily observed that my hourly wage was probably less than when I was in graduate school, which is hard to imagine. I was working down the pay scale.

MEET THEM WITH YOUR HEART READY TO BREAK

So it's easy to get discouraged. Now that I've been an activist and teacher for a long time, I survey the conditions on the ground. In our profession, half of us will leave before we've taught for 5 years, because the work is too hard, too lonely, too bureaucratic, too isolating—and it often involves kids. (Oh crap! I forgot about that!)

It's also a low self-esteem sector. If you're a student of history, you know that cultural protestations to the contrary (Ashley Judd says, in *People* magazine, that "teachers are heroes"), most Americans don't think much of the teaching profession, and never have. Back in the eighteenth century, teachers were hired off boats of incoming wanderers; the least able-bodied workers, the ones who showed an utter lack of entrepreneurial spirit and backbone—they became teachers. (I show my sophisticated undergraduate students the Walt Disney film of Ichabod Crane to get an idea.) In America, teaching traditionally has been a place where unmarried women went to "civilize" an unruly populace's children, as White people expanded westward, and later, to "give culture" to waves of immigrants from undesirable countries. Teaching has been a career where men ruled women (only lately has that changed even a little), where White people ruled everyone else, where adults ruled children, where kids dubbed "smart" ruled kids labeled "dumb." That, some have said, is exactly the point, except for those lucky enough or privileged enough not to go to schools like that.

There's also a lot of passive-aggressive behavior in our sector, fear of being found out that we're not good enough. More and more teachers are paid for performance, even when the measures are dubious at best; teachers endure working conditions that allow them little time for professional learning or collaboration; they teach scripted curricula; their school's test scores get published in the local newspaper. Teachers and administrators are still people who get critiqued for a lot of things over which they have no control, and then they complain bitterly among themselves but don't organize to change things or speak up. We have teachers' rooms aplenty, all around the country, that are outposts and hideouts for us-vs.-them talk, where administrators are hated, where kids are blamed, where professional dispossession and self-doubt can take root, if that kind of real stuff were talked about. I get a lot of e-mails from teachers who say, "I'm just about at my wits' end. I know I'm a good teacher, but I think I have to leave the profession. I just can't take it."

A person *could* get discouraged. What, you wanted an easy problem?

But in spite of everything I've just said, I'm not discouraged. (Wasn't it Winston Churchill who suggested that when you're in hell, just keep going?) Why, you may wonder?

Because there is the connection you have with your students. You know those students I had in my first years of teaching, even when I was a very inexperienced, very ambitious teacher who tried a lot of things that didn't work out so well? Well, I still hear from many of them. I meet with them in coffee shops, I talk with them about graduate school, I visit them when I travel around the country, they write me e-mails about their lives as teachers, and in some cases I've gone to their own classes to visit them (where they are doing some of the things I did, only much better). They tell me about how much they learned in those crazy, experimental, caring days and how different it was for them to be in a class where they were expected to cocreate the learning and to feel that what they had to say in class really mattered.

So it came to me finally that when you are fully, completely present to students, actually engaged in trying to understand their learning and also aware of the fact that you are learning alongside them, trying to get better at your work, oftentimes your students really do know that you care. They feel it; they meet your eyes; and they often, even in spite of their years of bad history with an institution that has roughed them up and told them they're not worth much, trust you and make themselves vulnerable. With sufficient craft and self-knowledge, you can make your classroom a safe space, where individuals can speak about their differences, where the strong do not tyrannize the weak, and where the privileged do not hold all the cards. If you're really interested in what your students are learning about, and you tell them that and meet them every morning with your heart ready to break, your students will eventually come to you in ways that you can't possibly imagine. And that, to me, is a small revolution every day. It keeps you going, through a lot of crappy stuff.

TOUGH-MINDED OPTIMISM

Now I work almost full-time at "reforming" school culture. I go around the country and talk with teachers about why the institution acts as it does, and what they can do about it. I encourage them to take heart and to be activists, to name the dysfunctional parts of school culture and to stand up and be troublemakers. (Although not everyone is cut out for it, I really do love troublemakers.) I often remind teachers of the importance of "tough-minded optimism," and the need to stick with it, like a mule, even when conditions seem very inauspicious.[1] I remind people that "Peace is not the absence of conflict. It is the presence of justice," as Dr. Martin Luther King, Jr., said. I also remind myself to be thankful for all the visionary teachers and mentors I've had, the ones who brought ideas like these to my own life.

I take heart in this kind of action. I think action and activism to make our profession better, wherever we find ourselves in the teaching and education world, breed optimism and vitality. The only thing to do, when we find ourselves overwhelmed and depressed, is to admit that we feel this way—and then to do something about it.

As a young teacher, your mettle will be tested. You will wonder why you decided to do this thankless work in this blank snake pit with people who don't seem to share your values or insights. Or you will work for the worst boss in the world—dysfunctional, overcontrolling, incompetent—and you will see that she is scared out of her mind and feels totally overwhelmed. There will be challenges from children, young adults, parents, your colleagues. Your classes will vex you, tire you, and misunderstand you. Your exquisitely crafted lessons, those you stayed up until 2 in the morning working on, will fall upon blank faces and dead classroom air, and you will glance down panicked at your watch and wonder how long this will go on until you are set free into your own self-judging hell.

But you will also meet incandescent souls in your classrooms, children and young adults whose lives change you forever because of the stories they tell you about themselves, and the things they teach you (if you let them). You may be regarded as an innovator, a maverick, a crazy person, and yet, if you are there, present to the soul connection of your students and some particular colleagues, this work will feed you and challenge you like nothing else. That, in my mind, is pretty much the best deal there is.

And what, you wanted an easy problem?

NOTE

1. "Both the tough-mindedness and the optimism are immensely important. We need to believe in ourselves, but not to believe that life is easy. Nothing in the historical record tells us that triumph is assured. But the future is shaped by men and women with a steady, even zestful, confidence that on balance their efforts will not have been in vain. They take failure and defeat not as reason to doubt themselves, but as reason to strengthen resolve. Some combination of hope, vitality and indomitability makes them willing to bet their lives on ventures of unknown outcome. . . . Second, I would emphasize staying power. Stamina is an attribute rarely celebrated by the poets, but it has had a good deal to do with the history of humankind. And with the life history of each person. Nothing is ever finally safe. We need a hard-bitten morale that enables us to face these truths and still strive with every ounce of our energy to prevail." Gardner (1995, pp. 127–128).

REFERENCES

Gardner, J. (1995). *Self-renewal: The individual and the innovative society* (pp. 127–128). New York: W.W. Norton.
Rich, M. (2009, August 29). A new assignment: Pick books you like. *New York Times*. http://www.nytimes.com/2009/08/30/books/30reading.html?_r=2&pagewanted=1

Chapter 16

It's Not on the Test: A Search for Existential Meaning in Three Acts

CHRISTOPHER L. DOYLE

ALMOST A QUARTER CENTURY TEACHING and two themes stand out: irony and faith. This sounds ironic in itself, because irony is often a stance of disenchanted souls who have lost faith. In *The Great War and Modern Memory,* Paul Fussell (1975) identifies irony as characteristic of the twentieth century and cites the First World War as the reason for its ascendance. Naive patriotism and innocence gave way to pointless carnage and disillusionment. Anyone who has read Ernest Hemingway will understand the kind of postwar-postmodern-ironic outlook Fussell has in mind.

Living the first forty years of my life in the Ironic Century was great preparation for teaching history to 16-year-olds. My students operate in a popular culture that trivializes the past, flattens its complexity, or writes it off as irrelevant, as illustrated by the put-down: "Him? Oh, he's history." Historian Eric Hobsbawm (1994) sees eeriness in this culture and says that young people now "grow up in a sort of permanent present lacking any organic relation to the public past of the times they live in" (p. 3). It takes creativity, tact, humor, and luck to make headway against such a state. The armor of irony helps, too, especially when a lesson goes awry.

Still, I've learned how to draw in these adolescents. Even more wondrous, over the years I've seen some highly unlikely students transfigured by learning. Given the right moment, subject, and enthusiasm, transfiguration can happen anywhere. My faith in this miracle has deepened by seeing it occur in gritty, neglected institutional settings among people who had every right to be overwhelmed by everyday burdens of living. It even happened to me.

ACT I, 1985

Three years out of college, I was clueless. By default, I had taken my father's advice and gotten a job in sales; to be precise, selling carpet to guys who owned Persian rug shops in Washington, D.C. I bought a Porsche and developed an extravagant habit of going out to nightclubs four or five nights a week. I chatted up girls, worked out at the gym, and met other people my age doing more or less the same. Some even liked it.

Exiting a dance club one night, maybe it was early morning, I swear the place was called "Poseurs," I walked up Wisconsin Avenue in Georgetown and fumbled for my car keys as it started raining. The wind kicked up from the Potomac and blew garbage out of the gutter. It stuck to me.

Over the next couple of days, I called my former college advisor, put in a rare appearance at church, and phoned my parents to tell them I was thinking of becoming a teacher. My dad said I was crazy for turning my back on a well-paying job. But my old professor was encouraging and mentioned that I didn't need a certificate to teach in private schools. The priest I bumped into after mass helped, too.

I ended up taking the priest to lunch, not something my 24-year-old self had ever imagined doing before. Over coffee, I gave him a brief story of my life, told him I wanted to do something worthwhile, and confessed to a fear I'd end up married, a father, and trapped in a job I hated: an angry breadwinner.

"Maybe you've got a calling to be a teacher, Chris." The priest said he knew about callings. "In any case, there's nothing wrong with wanting to live your own life." That line stayed with me.

Six months later I was back in Connecticut, my home state, driving my Porsche with a "For Sale" sign in the back window to my $13,000-a-year Catholic high school teaching job. I'd return each afternoon to the third-floor walkup I shared with a law student, run, grab dinner, and trudge up the hill past the state capitol building, offices, and Bushnell Hall, to the Hartford Public Library on Main Street.

There, I would spend 2 to 4 hours most nights grading papers and planning desperately to stay one class period ahead of my students. Teaching U.S. history wasn't too bad, at least I knew something about it, but psychology was brutal. Everything I remembered from "Psych I" spilled out the first day of school, with time to spare, and then I improvised with "Why don't we all introduce ourselves?" My history degree allegedly qualified me to teach everything from oedipal complexes to microeconomics and the *Marbury v. Madison* case. I had a lot to learn before I could teach anything passably well.

I checked out histories of psychology, textbooks, Freud's works and Jung's, the behaviorists, books on human development and personality, the *Diagnostic and Statistical Manual of Mental Disorders*, case studies of mental illnesses, and depictions of famous experiments from Pavlov to Milgram. I usually selected a work or two of history as well, to bone up on whatever I happened to be teaching at the moment in my U.S. history classes. The librarians were saints; they helped me and all the other patrons, including the homeless people who frequented the city library on cold evenings.

Some of those homeless were remarkably well read. Seeing someone down on his luck poring over *Finnegans Wake* contributed to the Great Humbling I experienced all year. My college degree didn't mean I knew anything; certainly not about living on the streets, or James Joyce, or even the subjects I taught. In the stacks, I felt like a novice penitent working on my faith alongside other disciples whose poverty lent them a gravity and conviction far beyond my own.

I lived within walking distance of four great libraries and used them all: the public, Trinity College, UConn Law School, and the Connecticut State Library. I had chosen to live in Hartford under the greatly mistaken impression that it might offer a Georgetown-on-the-cheap social life. The dearth of downscale D.C.-like partying was offset by the lucky accident of getting a fine means of self-education at my doorstep.

Still, I wasn't good in the classroom that first year. My students were patient. One or two were brilliant and put my own high school self to shame. I sometimes read aloud in class from books I enjoyed, which kids liked, but I didn't ask nearly enough questions, didn't let them run things, debate, role-play, define their own research problems, teach lessons, or have a say about class organization and content. I spent mind-numbing hours writing comments on their essays, which they seemed rarely to read. The grade, I guess, was what they noticed.

Broke, I used the school's weight room instead of a health club and in the process got better acquainted with some students who were gym rats. Two of them could have been stand-up comics; we laughed a lot. I heard from another one day about his parents' divorce. Reagan was president, and he had yet to be invented as an iconic savior by the right. The gym rats and I dismissed him as a lightweight. We debated the history of the Cold War, the decline of the West, and whether the assistant principal was a "complete jerk," as they swore he was. These conversations were richer than anything I got in class.

I lived on macaroni and cheese, peanut butter and jelly, and cafeteria lunches. I heard there might be layoffs before the next year, which turned out to be true and cost me my job, so in the spring I started classes toward public school certification. The Porsche went, replaced by an oil-guzzling, rusty Pontiac. I lived more frugally than I ever had and was busier and more tired than ever.

To an acquaintance, the teaching life seemed a comedown from my carpet-selling Georgetown days. My Pontiac "sucked," she told me. My social sphere had contracted, too. I was making less than a third of my previous salary, living in a marginal neighborhood, and my relationship with my parents was strained. It also felt frustrating to keep hitting my limits as a teacher.

Yet what I was doing felt pure. Teaching became my existential answer. It would be a lie to say it was for my students' sakes. It was about me. It would also be false to claim I had a calling to teach;

I was not a natural, and the few talents I did have required lots of cultivation. I was eager to keep cultivating, though. The subjects I taught probed the roots of humanity and suggested larger truths. No cloistered monk, nonetheless I was looking for something deep in those libraries.

ACT II, 1997

"Was slavery in the South a relic of traditional agrarian society and its values, or did it fit well with rising market capitalism?" I asked the question to 21 college undergraduates taking my History of American Slavery seminar.

"Masters didn't act like capitalists. They fought duels and took hunting trips to prove their manhood. They didn't play team sports like baseball. That's what Greenberg said, right?"

"Yeah, but they wanted their slaves to work efficiently. They taught them how to pay attention to the clock. They tried to teach them clock discipline. They wanted to maximize profits and efficiency. That sounds just like a factory boss."

"Isn't this guy we're reading now, Genovese, a Marxist? Isn't he saying that labor in the Old South is comparable to labor in any capitalist system?"

I listened to three of my students—Ernestine, Duquall, and Brian—debate with a sophistication that 2 months ago I never would have thought possible. The venue was a small, down-on-its-luck, manqué liberal arts college. Over time, the place had metamorphosed into a credentialing institution. It blended perfectly with the decaying landscape of the inner city in Western Massachusetts where it stands even now.

I worked as the unlikely head of its history program. Department meetings were a breeze, because I was the only full-time historian. I wrestled continually against the nagging thought that my place of employment and my particular niche in it were jokes—until I taught this class.

My students were mostly not history majors. They came from the business department, schools of education and nursing, even the atrophied philosophy program. At the outset, I wondered how such an assortment would take to the reading and writing I assigned. I had studied slavery in grad school. My doctoral dissertation explored some of its complexities. With all the fervor of a young scholar, I studded the course syllabus with books I thought were important or engaging. I came to each session with a list of questions about the readings, listened to students' answers, and then asked them to lead their own discussions. I gave them each an additional article or two, and they taught their classmates. It worked.

I came to know and admire them. Ernestine had heard stories about ancestors who were slaves and wanted to learn more about the "peculiar institution" that loomed large in family history. She was a nurse in training who made time for our class while interning nights at a city hospital.

Duquall wanted to be a high school principal. All idealism, he planned to return to his native South Carolina and lead a school system. Not well off, he had turned down admission to better schools to accept a football scholarship at ours. Taking this tough class coinciding with football season, he started at fullback on our winning Division II team.

Brian was similarly situated. He aspired to teach history, read incessantly, and was a shrewd student of pop culture. Inclined to studiousness, Brian relied on his soccer scholarship to pay for school. He likened athletic commitments to a job.

Scholarship athletes are often the worst students, but here they were among the best. Hardly anything worked as I imagined it should at this place. I was a newly minted Ph.D., yet my job title read "Assistant Professor of History and Department Chair."

Like my students, I ended up here because I needed money. This was the only job going. When I began work at the college, Bev and I had been married for 7 years. She encouraged me through the M.A. degree that I completed nights and summers, and then she supported me when I left high school teaching for full-time graduate study at the University of Connecticut. Upon graduation, I found myself with two kids, a mortgage, and a very tired spouse who brought in almost all our income. I needed a job.

But about the realities of academic job-hunting, I remained a near-hopeless naïf who was ignorant, at first, even to the fact that most people pursued doctorates because they intended to work as university professors. I loved history and had entertained vague notions of returning to high school teaching. As my professors reoriented me, I began to flatter myself with visions of the professorate and the Ivy League.

Such fantasies were complicated by the fact that historians are a dime a dozen. The job market was so crowded that applicants relocated anywhere for work. Universities were flush with résumés and posted job ads like this: "The successful candidate will be able to teach U.S. labor history, have a secondary field in eighteenth-century Latin America, will have published a book, and will be able to direct the Women's Studies program" (I am not making this up). They actually found people who fit any description they could dream up.

I should have been suspicious when my thesis advisor told me he'd received a call from the head of the history department at this school "practically in your backyard, Chris." They had circumvented the usual route of job postings in the trade papers, cattle-call interviews at the annual meeting of the American Historical Association, and asking two or three finalists to campus to interview and teach classes. They wanted to hire someone local, without a big search.

As it turned out, they didn't want to spend the money such a search required, and if they had, it is unlikely that any distant finalists would have relocated, poor market notwithstanding, to work in such a place. I kept ignoring the warning signals this too-good-to-be true interview was so clearly sending.

I did so because I had no options. The pay was awful, and the president of the college seemed like a character out of a Stanley Kubrick film: a chain-smoking accountant with the personal warmth of Doctor Strangelove. But his offer of employment meant health and retirement benefits, as well as whatever security came at such a place with the tenure track.

My new office was on the second floor of a Gilded Age mansion the college had taken over. It needed renovation urgently. I cajoled maintenance to paint the office and a sitting room used, I imagined, decades ago for seminars and coffees. Pictures of old-time history faculty studded the walls; books they wrote back in the 1960s, covered in dust, were displayed on shelves. Looking at black-and-white photos from when there had actually been a viable history program, I thought of that resort hotel and the pictures of its long-dead guests that drove Jack Nicholson crazy in *The Shining*. Nothing left here but me and ghosts.

I wore a jacket and tie, always, to suggest professionalism. I observed an adjunct teach a history class. He lacked training and basic knowledge in history, and he condescended to students. He had gotten the job because he worked as an administrator at the college, wanted to teach, and no one had thought to look elsewhere for faculty. I refused to let him have a class the following term or any other. Since he managed maintenance, he told me I could forget about further work involving history offices.

I streamlined the curriculum, added methods and non-Western-history requirements, and recruited part-time faculty with advanced degrees in history. I taught four classes a term and tried, not too successfully, to do a little writing. Some of the history majors complained I graded too hard. Surreptitiously, I took the test Massachusetts required of aspiring public school history teachers. My majors would have to pass said test to get work in their preferred career field; it was tough, requiring factual recall, interpretive flair, and writing skills—there were essays. I didn't lower my standards and lost some students, but others signed on, and the program grew overall.

The job was a struggle, but this class on slavery, at that crazy school, in my hectic life, was the best teaching experience I ever had. We ate lunch together, my students and I, on the last day of the term. The oldest was about 60, the youngest was 19. Over soup, I confessed to them my amazement at how well they had done. "Your discussions were on par with anything I heard in grad school; your insights were penetrating; your writing kept improving; and our time together flew by. Let me in on the secret. Why did it work so well? What do you think? How can I replicate this in the future?"

Ernestine said, "We really wanted to be here. You knew the subject, and you listened to us. We could tell you cared. . . . But, I don't think you'll get students like us very often. I think maybe we spoiled you." She was right.

We were all overscheduled and worried about the same litany of family, money, and our futures. We suffered institutional neglect. I remember asking Brian about campus life, and his response was, "We live in poverty in the dorms." I sensed that many of us used our commitment to the class as a coping mechanism. We threw ourselves into the books, ideas, and writing, and we tuned out the other stuff. The subject matter came with its own gravity, too, and it pulled us in.

I read once that Malcolm X found prison the perfect place to get an education. We weren't in jail, but this class confirmed that the life of the mind can be cultivated anywhere, by anyone, no matter what life throws at us. Perhaps, like Malcolm and those hard-luck patrons I encountered a dozen years earlier at the Hartford Public Library, we discovered that austerity focused us and led us to search.

I began to see other truths that had appeared only as dim impressions as a new teacher. Knowing my subject did, in fact, matter. My students respected my expertise, and that helped me relax and focus on them. My teaching had moved much closer to the conversational style I once enjoyed with the gym rats. The slavery class was a seminar; we shared a passion and enjoyed talking about it. There was little sense of hierarchy and no pressure to impress or score an A grade. We felt enthusiasm. It was electric.

ACT III, 2009

I am giving the commencement speech at the suburban public high school where I teach. In front of me sit some 350 capped-and-gowned seniors, parents, relatives, colleagues, administrators, and my own two kids. Emma, 17, is just a year away from her graduation. Lee, almost 14, would rather be almost anywhere than listening to the old man drone on at a boring ceremony. I stand on a makeshift dais in the middle of the football field. A breeze and low humidity temper the late-afternoon sun. I talk about finding the parts of yourself that make you the most uncomfortable, the parts you want to bury or repress, what Carl Jung called the "shadow self."

I cite students in the crowd and how they looked for their shadow selves in projects that took them in unexpected directions. A pacifist flower child I had taught opted to study young people who enlist in the military. One of those enlistees, an idealistic young man in the same class, researched atrocities committed by Americans fighting the War on Terror. As they studied, something attracted both of them to their antitheses.

I invoke historical examples: two Philadelphia Quakers from the early 1700s who were intent on purchasing slaves, until their shadow selves brought them horrific nightmares about slavery. The pair went on to become two of the first abolitionists. "They found their best selves. But first they had to find their real selves," I conclude. "Maybe in these uncertain times, all we can count on is ourselves. In any case, you won't be much good to anyone else unless you take care of yourselves." I realized, after the fact, that I was channeling the priest's advice from 24 years earlier.

These students' shadow selves cry for attention. Over the past year, they had given the principal fits by turning a pep rally into a striptease, writing antiauthoritarian articles in the school paper, "grinding" at dances, and not taking Advanced Placement exams seriously. Yet most of them, the ones I know, had expended considerable effort striving for admission to prestigious colleges.

I taught about 70 of them in Humanities classes and had gotten them to read Dostoyevsky's *Notes from Underground*, some Nietzsche, chunks of *Anna Karenina*, Michel Foucault, Camus's *The Stranger*, and other works in an existential vein. These kids simultaneously fought and played to the institutional ideal. They had curiosity and could be seduced into deep thinking, but they were also intent on buffing their résumés and tweaking authority.

They identified with me because I helped them critique the milieu they found so problematic, but I also graded their work and taught them to succeed at the very tests they complained about. I shared their frustrations and reservations about the place, but I ran the risk of becoming "The Man" who enforced the rules. Probably, my own shadow self could use attention.

Norms of public education and adolescence had changed dramatically since my last foray into secondary teaching. It wasn't only the No Child Left Behind law and its reductionist focus on standardized tests. Middle-class childhood has become a project, an extension of parental and community status anxiety. There are undoubtedly larger reasons for this stress. In *The Rise and Fall of the Great Powers*, historian Paul Kennedy (1987) reveals the striking similarity between modern American fears of decline and the same worry in Edwardian England a century ago. In both cases, young people felt the fallout in the form of educational "reform" emphasizing standards, competitiveness, and efficiency.

At first, it startled me how pace, pressure, and test numbers defined the school. My Advanced Placement students were terrifically overscheduled. "When did you get to sleep last night?" I began asking. The answers were discouraging: midnight, 1, 2. A cadre of the "best and brightest" text-messaged late on school nights, often until 3 a.m. Staying up to do homework and text each other indicated membership in the club of highest achievement.

Students who took three to six Advanced Placement classes, played sports, and competed on robotics teams and at music recitals almost always turned to cheating as a survival tactic. In fact, cheating was rampant among all students. I inquired about it, and kids were surprisingly honest. They copied homework (the most frequent form of dishonesty), cribbed on tests (second-most-favored tactic), and cut and pasted text from Web sites into their writing. Two kids told me they misused Adderall, a medication prescribed for attention deficit disorder, as a study-enhancing drug to help with focus and memorization.

They have different ways of rationalizing cheating. Some claim it is a by-product of thoughtless pedagogy. "We aren't going to respect teachers who give us photocopied worksheets as busy work. We're not going to spend time doing that kind of homework." Others call it "sticking it to The Man" who compels them to overwork. Still others assert that "as long as we do well on the tests, the homework doesn't matter." The savviest students denigrated crude plagiarism. "It's stupid to get caught lifting text from the Internet. No one should be doing that," because it lacks subtlety.

However, even strident defenders of cheating admit it is bad. If the school worked better, they wouldn't do it, they say. Quite a few express sentiments of guilt, and I feel bad for them. The system sends a lot of implicit messages that what they are doing is okay. They believe they have to turn their backs on their moral sensibilities in order to succeed. It makes them cynical.

I teach classes at both ends of the academic spectrum. We "track" students based on teachers' and guidance counselors' assessments of their ability. Often, the "low-level" classes are populated by kids from the poorer parts of town or from a nearby city—a small group of kids get bused in to promote integration. These kids have a healthier approach to limiting schoolwork, making time for friends and family, and enjoying themselves. But they are marginalized from the school mainstream and act like they know it.

The focus on test success makes teaching and learning too narrow. When I asked my department chair why Advanced Placement students in U.S. History did not write term papers, he responded, "This is a test prep class. We don't have time for research." I have had better success implementing such assignments in "lower-level" history classes, but I am an exception to the norm.

Instruction comes to a halt frequently so we can test the entire school: a week of midterm exams, another week of finals, 2 weeks of state-mandated standardized tests, a day for in-school PSATs for 10th and 11th graders, 2 weeks of Advanced Placement testing (over 60% of students take at least one AP class, and many take more than that). It can be difficult to find time for concerted thinking.

Yet students still want to follow their passions. Jamie asked if I would moderate a chess club he wanted to start. "We just want to use your room, put on some music, and play," and they do, every week. They are the least competitive and most sportsmanlike players of the game I have ever seen.

Another bunch wanted me to oversee their bicycling club. We take to the roads every Friday, weather permitting. They are the

Keystone Cops of cycling: flat tires, badly fitting machines, going full-out and then blowing spectacularly into anaerobic deficit, "bonking" from no food or water on long rides. But when we get back to school, all they talk about was how much fun it was and how "next week, we should do a longer ride."

They particularly love field trips. Humanities students told me that "the best day of high school was when we went to see Momix," a modern dance troupe whose directors I know. We got to see a dress rehearsal Momix performed at a beautiful old Art Deco theater. "Yeah, and it was even better when we went to that coffeehouse afterward. We got to talk, and some of the dancers came in and we spoke with them. Remember?" I doubt I could devise a standardized measure of assessing this kind of joy.

Some students fall in love with history, philosophy, literature, and art. One of my Humanities students, a Korean immigrant, undertook a yearlong study of "faith in the writings of Leo Tolstoy." Another kid opted for an independent study of "the development of capitalistic values in the early-modern Western world." His final paper and presentation were on par with what an advanced undergraduate might have done. A talented musician and pianist studied "innovation in the music of Claude Debussy" after I invoked the French composer when we studied creativity. Passion and enthusiasm carry them, just as those qualities worked with my college students of slavery.

A gentle touch, the right material, humor, and direct questions get these kids. It's best to start by asking about them: their interests, experiences, and frustrations. I am fighting a trend in education whereby kids are subjects to be operated on and "improved."

When I was hired, the superintendent of schools told all the new teachers, "We have a great school system, but as newcomers you might see things that need improving. If you do, let us know." My second year, I took him at his word and worked my way up the chain of command, expressing concern about the cheating, overemphasis on testing, and tracking. They were all related, I said, and they led us to miss larger purposes of education. Worse, they encouraged students' bad ethical choices.

My bosses disagreed. Some said I was too focused on "outliers." Others asserted that the pros of our school, good test scores and college acceptance rates, outweighed the cons. Another claimed that "the community wants it this way" and wouldn't tolerate anything else. They chalked up cheating to a larger problem in American culture. I replied that we could either reinforce or work against larger trends. My supervisor let me know that if I persisted with such criticism, I would lose my job.

This is in many ways the toughest place I have worked, yet I have stayed here longer than any other job I have held. After all that studying, I no longer see myself as a historian. I haven't written academic history or taught college in years. But I am growing increasingly comfortable acting subversively and using history to help students find themselves.

To that end, I develop the lessons my students remember best. I teach about the imposition of clocks, the forced cultivation of time discipline, and an increasing emphasis on efficiency at the expense of humanity that occurred in the late 1700s and 1800s. I teach about a style of child rearing, originating with John Locke's *Some Thoughts Concerning Education* (1692/2000), in which parents cultivate affectionate ties with their children and then manipulate those ties to secure obedience. The historian Philip Greven (1977) has shown how such conditionally affectionate families operate and how they contribute to making kids insecure and neurotic; my students read his work. I teach about individuals and groups who, for resisting their superiors' impersonal demands to work hard and be productive, were diagnosed with mental disorders, as doctors in the antebellum South labeled chronically runaway slaves "drapetomanic." The point is that repressing the self has a cost, but people can fight back, and sometimes they overcome resistance and find their best selves.

This is at the core of my teacher's faith: Unless we are terribly damaged, we all want to be transfigured. A part of us desires desperately to find existential meaning. I cling to the belief that any classroom has potential to be sacred ground. Distilling education down to mere technical skills, grades, or (worse still) status competition blasphemes.

This faith gets me out of bed when the alarm goes off Monday mornings. Hearing from students who say I've made a difference, seeing my own kids becoming the unique best selves they have the potential to be, the faith seems justified. Maybe teaching has become my calling.

REFERENCES

Fussell, P. (1975). *The great war and modern memory.* New York: Oxford University Press.

Greven, P. (1977). *The Protestant temperament, patterns of child rearing, religious experience, and the self in early America.* New York: Knopf.

Hobsbawm, E. (1994). *The age of extremes: A history of the world, 1914–1991.* New York: Pantheon Books.

Kennedy, P. (1987). *The rise and fall of the great powers: Economic change and military conflict from 1500 to 2000.* New York: Random House.

Locke, J. (2000). *Some thoughts concerning education.* New York: Oxford University Press. (Original work published 1692)

Chapter 17

From Surviving to Thriving

SONIA NIETO

T O REMAIN ENTHUSIASTIC AND COMMITTED in their work, teachers need environments that promote meaningful learning. How do teachers move from simply surviving to actively thriving in the profession? How do they go from dreading the trials and tribulations that each day brings to instead welcoming the challenges awaiting them?

Having been a classroom teacher myself (as well as the wife of one teacher and the mother of another), I know it takes a great deal of dedication to walk into school every day with enthusiasm, energy, and love, often in spite of conditions that make doing so a constant struggle. Yet some teachers do it all the time, and many remain in the classroom for years with a commitment that is nothing short of inspirational. These teachers (including my husband and daughter) have been the source of my admiration as well as much of my work. Throughout the years, I have explored the question of why and how they do it.

WHY DO WE TEACH?

My research has made it clear that previous experiences as well as values, dispositions, and beliefs fuel teachers' determination to remain in the profession. Sensibilities such as love, engaging with intellectual work, the hope of changing students' lives, a belief in the democratic potential of public education, and anger at the conditions of public education are all at the heart of what makes for excellent and caring teachers (Nieto, 2003). Attitudes and values such as a sense of mission; solidarity with, and empathy for, students; the courage to challenge mainstream knowledge and conventional wisdom; improvisation; and a passion for social justice are teachers' motivations for entering the profession (Nieto, 2005).

On the other hand, teachers have never mentioned to me that teaching students how to take tests, learning to follow rubrics and templates, or heeding district mandates concerning the latest basal reader helped to keep them in the classroom or made teaching a rewarding experience. Although these tools and techniques may be helpful, truly "highly qualified teachers" have never viewed them as ends in themselves.

My experience has shown me that a number of conditions sustain teachers' energy and commitment to keep going. These include policies and practices at the school and district levels and attitudes and actions on the part of teachers themselves.

SCHOOL AND DISTRICT CONDITIONS

Because of state licensing requirements, all teachers must engage in professional development both before they enter the profession and periodically afterward. In spite of such requirements, too often teachers find that their professional development is both inadequate and irrelevant. For example, a survey of more than 5,000 teachers concerning their preparedness to teach found that fewer than 45% had participated in professional development programs focused on teaching students of diverse cultural backgrounds; worse still, only 26% had any training at all in working with students of diverse language backgrounds (Parsad, Lewis, & Farris, 2001). Yet the reality is that students of color and those for whom English is a second language go to school in every city and state. They are found increasingly in rural districts, and in many places, they are the majority.

In addition, in spite of the ineffectiveness of short-term and whole-school professional development activities, these kinds of programs remain ubiquitous in schools. Mandated professional development activities—in which administrators select the topics and teachers are a captive audience for a half or whole day—are notoriously unproductive. The result is often frustration and resentment on the part of teachers, dissatisfaction on the part of administrators, and a fruitless allocation of scarce resources.

GIVE TEACHERS CHOICES

Probably the most significant action school districts can take in changing the nature of professional development is to provide meaningful and engaging programs that respect the intelligence and good will of teachers and help them grow in terms of knowledge, awareness, and practice. Such professional development is characterized by teachers' ability to select the topics they want to learn more about and the opportunity to work collaboratively with colleagues.

For instance, in a yearlong inquiry group with high school teachers in Boston, Massachusetts, Stephen Gordon (2003), a veteran teacher of English, wrote about his frustration with the traditional character of professional development:

> I am not looking for prescriptions for teachers. I am not looking for narrow "silver-bullet" programs that script teacher behaviors using some quasi-scientific rationale. I want to find ways to teach that embody the several theories and beliefs that I have come to believe are true and good, truths and knowledge that have consequence for educating urban children. I can do little about the injustice and racism that permeate our institutions. I want to create pedagogy that makes me feel I have done my best. (p. 86)

ENCOURAGE PARTNERSHIPS

Districts and universities can support meaningful research opportunities by providing long-term collaborations that enable teachers to earn master's degrees or professional development units. One example is the Access to Critical Content and English Language Acquisition (ACCELA) Alliance (see http://www.umass.edu/accela), a joint project with the Springfield and Holyoke Public Schools in Massachusetts in which I was involved with my colleagues at the University of Massachusetts, Amherst. The goal was for regular classroom teachers to learn about, and develop strategies for working with, English language learners, most of whom were Latino. Most of the classrooms in both school districts included students who were learning English, and in some of these classrooms, they were actually in the majority. Yet most teachers had received little, if any, previous training in working with this population or in building relationships with their students' families.

ACCELA provided courses, technical assistance, and research opportunities for teachers to learn more about their students, as well as about language and literacy development, children's literature, and family outreach (Gebhard & Willett, 2008). The individual or joint research in which teachers engaged resulted in projects in which teachers not only honed their skills, but also developed greater confidence in working with students who were learning English. In the process, they learned about the sociocultural realities of Latino children and families and about teaching students effectively despite the strains of living in poverty. When teachers learned new ways of working with English language learners, the results ranged from improved student math skills to increased advocacy on the part of students as demonstrated by, among other activities, writing petitions to reclaim recess (Gebhard, Habana Hafner, & Wright, 2004; Gebhard, Harman, & Seger, 2007). Even more significant, many teachers developed strong relationships with families that will, in the long run, improve the education outcomes for their students.

FOSTER AN OPEN CLIMATE

Another important condition that encourages teachers to remain in the profession is a climate of openness, shared decision-making, and collaboration in the school. This means respecting the fact that teachers are professionals who may not always agree with administrators. Although it can be difficult for principals to have in their schools teachers who challenge their policies and practices, this approach is usually more constructive than running a school like a small fiefdom in which teachers have little say and feel they are treated more as technicians than as professionals.

Seth Peterson (2005), a high school English teacher in Boston, wrote about the seeming contradiction of working for openness and change in a system that is often bureaucratic and closed:

> My fellow teachers work in a system that trusts and expects them to know how to respond to a suicidal student, a bomb threat, or a hate crime. Yet this same system does not trust them to design the final exam for their own course. They teach the glory of this nation's struggle for freedom and defense of individual rights and yet are asked to do so with a curriculum that is standardized so that government agencies can measure growth more efficiently. . . . We, who do this work, are caught in a conundrum, working within the system to create change. (pp. 163–164)

Another Boston high school teacher, Ambrizeth Lima (2005), wrote about why teachers need to learn to question—and to teach their students to do so as well:

> Part of learning is to question things that we take for granted, to discover issues that need to be debated, to uncover hidden realities that need to be transformed. The more we learn, the more burdened we are because it becomes our responsibility to bring that knowledge to others, to make it explicit, and to do something with it. (pp. 92–93)

It is sometimes difficult to create conditions in schools that promote dialogue, interaction, and collaboration, yet they can make a significant difference in retaining good teachers.

ACTIONS TEACHERS CAN TAKE

Teachers' attitudes, beliefs, values, and dispositions have a powerful influence on why teachers teach and why they remain in the profession in spite of difficult conditions that test their resolve. Certainly, there are many dispositions, which include the love of students and subject matter; a view of themselves as lifelong learners and intellectual workers; a deep commitment to social justice; comfort with uncertainty; endless patience; and, of course, a sense of humor.

But instead of focusing on dispositions, I want to discuss three necessary actions—or dispositions to actions—that need to flow from teachers' values.

Action 1: Learning About Themselves

A number of years ago, my colleagues and I interviewed several alumni of our teacher education program, which prepares all teachers, not just bilingual or English as a second language teachers, to work with language-minority students (Gebhard, Austin, Nieto, & Willett, 2002). One of them was Mary Ginley, a veteran teacher of 30 years, who had recently been selected Massachusetts Teacher of the Year.

Mary spoke about why it had been necessary for her to learn more about herself to become an effective teacher of students who were different from her—and about how, for some teachers, this can be a difficult step:

> I went to a conference, and this teacher said to me, "1 don't understand you! What is all this multicultural stuff? Why can't we talk about how we are the same?" And I said to her, "The problem is when we do that, we are talking about how everybody is like us—White, middle-class, and monolingual." I know she didn't get it, but you have to step outside of yourself . . . and it takes a lot of energy to bridge that cultural gap. (Gebhard, Austin, et al., 2002, p. 233)

Mary decided that her learning had to begin with an awareness and reassessment of who she was, an examination of the unearned privileges she had as a White teacher of mostly students of color, and her unexamined preconceptions of the community in which she was teaching. She threw herself wholeheartedly into this work because she knew that her effectiveness as a teacher of children of backgrounds different from her own depended on her doing so.

Action 2: Learning About Their Students

Being open and willing to learn about their students is a key component of teachers' learning. But this does not mean simply reading a book on cultural differences or adding a unit on different family traditions. Although these can be helpful activities, they may do little to inform teachers about the students in their classrooms.

Teachers need to learn about the sociocultural realities of their students and the sociopolitical conditions in which they live. The late Brazilian educator Paulo Freire (1998) addressed this question eloquently when he wrote,

> Educators need to know what happens in the world of the children with whom they work. They need to know the universe of their dreams, the language with which they skillfully defend themselves from the aggressiveness of their world, what they know independently of the school, and how they know it. (pp. 72–73)

A good example comes from Juan Figueroa, a young Boston public high school teacher who knew "what happens in the world of the children" because he shared similar experiences as an urban student. Juan said,

> These kids were me. You know, I grew up in the city too, and that's what keeps me going. All the other stuff you had was crazy, but it's when you make that one-to-one connection with a kid, and a kid finally says, "Now I get it!" that makes everything else seem so right. (quoted in Nieto, 2003, p. 42)

Knowing "what happens in the world of the children" is also necessary for teachers who do not share the realities of their students. Mary Cowhey, a first- and second-grade teacher, makes it her business to learn about her students before the first day of class. For many years, I have asked students in an education course I teach to write a letter to Freire explaining how his ideas had influenced them and their practice (Nieto, 2008). Mary wrote,

> You write about reading the class. I guess I jump the gun. Part of how I address my fear about the first day of school is to face it, as you suggest. I spend the week before the first day of school visiting my students' homes, meeting the students and their families. I can't wait for the first day of school, and so I go out and read the students in their neighborhoods, their homes, with their families. That way I know where my students are coming from, literally. I know who their people are. I know the names their families call them. I know what they are proud of and what worries them. I begin to trust these families. My students and their families begin to trust me. (Cowhey, 2005, p. 13)

According to Mary, her August visits to students' homes are the best investment she makes all year because this is how she begins to really know her students.

Action 3: Developing Allies

Novice teachers often ask me for advice to help them get through their first year of teaching. My answer always is, "Make a friend." By this I mean that they should work to create a community because teaching, besides being tremendously difficult, can also be an incredibly lonely profession. I have found that when teachers develop allies, they remain fresh, committed, and hopeful.

Stephen Gordon (2003), one of the teachers in the Boston inquiry group, stressed the significance of collaboration and relationship. I had asked the teachers in the group, most of whom were veteran teachers, to write a letter of advice to a new teacher. Stephen wrote,

> To survive and grow, I had to find colleagues who share my anger, hopes, beliefs, and assumptions about students and teaching. When I discuss my teaching with these caring colleagues, I work to specify

exactly what troubles me; I fight the fear that having problems means I am doing something wrong. Sharing difficult truths and emotions has been necessary for my personal and professional development. (p. 98)

After hearing Stephen read a particularly moving piece he wrote about the uncertainty of teaching, another teacher expressed a feeling that all the teachers in the group shared. "You can kind of see why lots of people don't do this [work]," she said. "It's so painful" (Nieto, 2003, p. 89). Yet this kind of collaborative work is necessary for teachers to learn and grow.

WHAT TEACHERS NEED

Taking these actions is essential for thriving in the classroom. Nevertheless, teachers cannot do it alone. They need the respect and support of administrators and policy makers, who nowadays sometimes treat teachers as little more than test-givers. Teachers also need the support of the general public, which seems to have lost its belief in the centrality of public education in a democratic society. Instead, there is often a general mean-spiritedness when it comes to teachers and students and an indiscriminate belief in privatization schemes.

In spite of the current climate, I have found that many of the most dedicated and caring teachers have a deep reverence for the significance of public education in a democratic society. Perhaps Jennifer Welborn (2005), a middle school science teacher, sums it up best. In an essay about why she teaches, Jennifer wrote,

> I may be naive, but I believe that what I do day in and day out does make a difference. Teachers do change lives forever. And I teach in public school because I still believe in public school. I believe that the purpose of public school, whether it delivers or not, is to give a quality education to all kids who come through the doors. I want to be a part of that lofty mission. The future of our country depends on the ability of public schools to do that. (p. 17)

Too many teachers are leaving the profession because the ideals that brought them to teaching are fast disappearing. In addition, the status of teachers has eroded tremendously in the past few decades, and the conditions in which they work are often trying. If we are to keep good teachers in the classroom, school administrators and policy makers, among others, need to find ways to create environments in which teachers can form strong collaborative relationships with their peers and in which they can continue to learn about themselves, their students, and their students' communities. Until these things happen, survival will be the most we can hope for. But survival is simply not good enough—for teachers, for their students, or for the United States. When teachers develop allies, they remain fresh, committed, and hopeful.

It takes a great deal of dedication to walk into school every day with enthusiasm, energy, and love.

REFERENCES

Cowhey, M. (2005). Reading the class. In S. Nieto (Ed.), *Dear Paulo: Letters from those who dare teach* (pp. 10–16). Boulder, CO: Paradigm.

Freire, P. (1998). *Teachers as cultural workers: Letters to those who dare teach.* Boulder, CO: Westview Press.

Gebhard, M., Austin, T., Nieto, S., & Willett, J. (2002). "You can't step on someone else's words": Preparing all teachers to teach language minority students. In Z. Beykont (Ed.), *The power of culture: Teaching across language difference* (pp. 219–243). Cambridge, MA: Harvard Educational Publishing Group.

Gebhard, M., Habana Hafner, A., & Wright, M. (2004). Teaching English language learners the language game of math. *Harvard Education Letter, 20*(6), 5–7.

Gebhard, M., Harman, R., & Seger, W. (2007). Reclaiming recess in urban schools: The potential of systemic functional linguistics for ELLs and their teachers. *Language Arts, 84*(5), 419–430.

Gebhard, M., & Willett, J. (2008). Supporting teacher learning and the academic literacy development of ELLs in changing times. *Journal of Staff Development, 29*(1), 41–45.

Gordon, S. (2003). Letter to a new teacher. In S. Nieto, *What keeps teachers going?* (pp. 97–99). New York: Teachers College Press.

Lima, A. (2005). Teaching as a spiritual journey. In S. Nieto (Ed.), *Why we teach* (pp. 87–96). New York: Teachers College Press.

Nieto, S. (2003). *What keeps teachers going?* New York: Teachers College Press.

Nieto, S. (Ed.). (2005). *Why we teach.* New York: Teachers College Press.

Nieto, S. (Ed.). (2008). *Dear Paulo: Letters from those who dare teach.* Boulder, CO: Paradigm.

Parsad, B., Lewis, L., & Farris, E. (2001). *Teacher preparation and professional development: 2000* (NCES 2001-088). Washington, DC: U.S. Department of Education, National Center for Education Statistics.

Peterson, S. (2005). Always another beginning. In S. Nieto (Ed.), *Why we teach* (pp. 156–165). New York: Teachers College Press.

Welborn, J. (2005). The accidental teacher. In S. Nieto (Ed.), *Why we teach* (pp. 15–22). New York: Teachers College Press.

Teachers:
Arsonists of the Best Kind

AUDREY A. FRIEDMAN

Education is not the filling of a pail, but the lighting of a fire.

—William Butler Yeats

TO CREATE AND SUSTAIN ORDINARY COMBUSTION, three factors, known as the *fire triangle*, are essential: oxygen, a fuel source, and heat (Peige, 1977). Arson is the deliberate tampering with one or more of these factors to create combustion. In examining critical elements that lead to effective educational reform, Cohen and Ball (1999) identify a *learning triangle* of factors that enhance capacity and interaction: teachers, students, and materials (including technologies). They argue that the relationship among these three variables contributes to capacity as "interactions among teachers and students around educational material" (p. 2) yield instruction. Context (classroom and school), which is omitted from the triangle, however, is also a critical variable of educational reform because classrooms vary extensively within schools and schools vary extensively within districts. Of the four variables—teacher, context, students, and pedagogy (which includes curriculum and instruction)—the teacher is the only variable that (a) interacts with and impacts all three variables; (b) can manipulate or "tamper with" (in the most positive way) all three; and (c) can enter and exit the triangle at the most auspicious moments. The context provides oxygen, students are the fuel source, and pedagogy

135

is heat, which leaves the teacher as arsonist, capable of creating extraordinary combustion. Thus the very best teacher is an arsonist who deliberately manipulates oxygen, fuel source, and heat to light fires that move students to act humanely, explore antithetical beliefs, share their realities, create a parabolic fugue, and tackle the difficult problems. The students in turn inspire these very teachers to share their love of subject, to resurrect Yeats, teach what is enduring, and tolerate the dissonance and messiness of teaching. The essays in this text are testament to those arsonists, teachers who remain *burned in* to enhancing the life chances of all they serve. Despite circumstances that are increasingly rife with pollutants that disorient and deprofessionalize, these arsonists negotiate the messiness of classroom practice through critical inquiry into self, practice, and scholarship. Love of subject, reverence for public education, profound intellect, and tough-minded optimism power a pedagogy that overcomes the noxious fumes of high-stakes testing, scripted curricula, and races that are impossible to win. Ignited by a belief in the human spirit and a commitment to humanity, they tamper with the tension between freedom and discipline, creating critical sparks that inspire students to think, learn, live humanely, and shine their most brilliant lights. Continually stoking fires, these arsonists care for the young and vulnerable, reach students' hearts and minds, bring arts and sciences to life, and motivate others to create and sustain extraordinary combustion.

AN ARSON INVESTIGATION

Knowledge always demands increase; it is like fire, which must first be kindled by some external agent, but will afterwards always propagate itself.

—Samuel Johnson

About 5 years ago a colleague and I explored how a purposeful sample of dedicated teachers negotiated personal and professional epistemologies and maintained the inspiration, dedication, and fire to teach. We wondered, "What self does each teacher bring to bear on teaching and learning?" We learned that passion for subject and students, deep knowledge of subject, theory, and pedagogy, and love of teaching and learning are "burned in" to the personal and professional lives of the best teachers. Critical observation, reflection, and action are integral to their decision-making not only in their personal lives but also in their professional lives; thus personal and professional epistemologies are inextricably linked. Mission pervades their total existence, and although the context changes, their epistemological codes do not. Here are their stories.

THEIR FIERY SELVES

The most powerful weapon on earth is the human soul on fire.

—E. M. Forster

On the second Wednesday in October 2005, seven teachers gathered around a table of food and drink to talk about their passion; they came to tell their stories about teaching. They ranged in years of teaching experience from 1 to 19; they are four females and three males; they are two elementary, one middle, and four high school teachers; they are Latino, African American, Afro-Caribbean, and White; they teach in different urban schools; they are a special needs educator, a regular educator, a bilingual/occupational/special educator, three English educators, and two science educators. When asked what they are passionate about, they share a fiery dedication to students, learning, giving, and life.

Catherine, in her third year as a first-grade, integrated-classroom teacher, responds, "I love my children; I love it when they are happy and excited because something has 'clicked' for them!"

Darnell, a 7-year veteran, ninth-grade science teacher who works with "reinstated expelled adolescents," echoes, "I'm passionate about helping my students build and improve knowledge about science and life!"

Mariela, a 19-year veteran, high school bilingual, occupational, and special educator, is "passionate about her belief and vision that every child can learn."

Ashante, a 10-year veteran, middle school science teacher, "loves the questions of science and invites his students to ask and if possible, find the answers to those questions."

Renna, a 5-year veteran, elementary school educator, who served as an aide for 11 years, wants "to make sure that her daughter and all daughters receive an education that challenges them to think and solve the problems recurring in education today."

Susan, an 11-year veteran, high school English teacher, is passionate about "maintaining high expectations especially for kids who are 'stuck.'"

Josh, the novice in the group, "loves literature and wants his students to love literature and the life lessons literature shows them."

All ignore the immediate, personal self and place students, subject, practice, and learning at the center of their passion and profession. All acknowledge students (the fuel source), classroom community (oxygen), and teaching and learning (heat) as integral to their vision and mission as teachers, learners, and people. Like arsonists, all are responsible for manipulating the elements of the learning triangle to kindle understanding, incite learning, and spark change.

KINDLED SPIRITS

In everyone's life, at some time, our inner fire goes out. It is then burst into flame by an encounter with another human being. We should all be thankful for those people who rekindle the inner spirit.

—Albert Schweitzer

A gratefulness for who they are, and who have mentored, inspired them, and lit their fires pervades their first conversations. Darnell smiles as he comments: "I am a blessed person . . . the eldest of five, a foster-father of three, and a grandfather of four beautiful grand daughters. . . . I am a product of a single-parent, fast-paced yet protective rearing, extended family nurtured, latchkey and inner-city project developed." Ashante observes, "I was raised believing and now practice: you will receive more with honey than vinegar and that it does not hurt to be kinder to others. . . . Therefore, I try to be a gentle man, but more importantly I try to treat folks better than how or what I expect or would like to be treated." Josh is grateful for "his education and the opportunity to listen to the experiences of seasoned teachers." Susan "appreciates the opportunity to talk about teaching with colleagues and to be part of research that studies teachers." Catherine is "comforted by the support she is receiving from others who have experienced the same dilemmas that she has." Mariela views her profession as a way "of giving back to her teachers who encouraged a non-English-speaking child to achieve, excel, and become a teacher" and a way "to motivate her students to learn and excel." Renna enjoyed "being an aide in her daughter's classroom so much that she decided to become a certified teacher" and "feels fulfilled by the hard work and opportunity to make positive change for her students." There is no regret among these teachers: They appreciate their beginnings; they love their work; they love their content; they love their students; they want for their students the rich opportunities they themselves have enjoyed. As Pierre Teilhard de Chardin (2002) hopes: "Someday, after mastering the winds, the waves, the tides, and gravity, we shall harness for God the energies of love, and then, for a second time in the history of the world, man will have discovered fire" (p. 11). For these educators their personal and professional lives are inextricably linked, each fueling the other; they have discovered, created, and continue to sustain the fire within themselves and in others.

PUTTING OUT FIRES

The thorn bush is the ancient barrier in the road. It must catch fire if you want to go further.

—Franz Kafka

For these teachers, November brings numerous "aha" moments in the guise of "thorn bushes" that need burning for progress to occur. Susan observes: "November is disillusionment on the teacher timeline—in September you go in refreshed and excited—by November, you feel down and aggravated and sleep deprived—goes to end of December." Yet she finds comfort in "throwing out lesson plans," because she now "knows and has relationships with the kids in her room" and can develop instruction "based on who is sitting in my room—that's comfort." For Susan, teaching is a relationship; her students provide the fuel for her teaching, which is only effective when she "knows" each element in her classroom and can adjust the heat to create the best type of combustion. Darnell's "bad week" is a result of grades—"grading kids was a tough thing. If I am not OK, then my students won't be OK." Students' poor grades disrupt his sense of efficacy, but he refuses to lower his standards and expectations, "want[ing] students to progress the same way he progresses personally." He elaborates that many of his students are repeaters who need him to be a "social worker, a psychologist, to work through their dilemmas while I work through mine." He knows that he must be more than a teacher "if his students [are] to be prepared for the next level."

Mariela feels increasing dissonance as she is "overwhelmed by the politics of things—prescriptive pedagogy conflicts with her beliefs and evidence." Her teaching partner has also felt overwhelmed by seeing "wonderful programs go down the tubes because of a lack of support: a very difficult obstacle to deal with in practice." To address this discomfort, she assumes the perspective of "mothers who hope to be good mothers and raise just and considerate children." Maternal instincts help ease the angst created by institutional structures that ignore evidence and conflict with her personal and professional beliefs. "Two pre-pracs were placed with a sub[stitute teacher]," Renna complains. "This is inappropriate for the students and the pre-pracs!" She went to the principal to straighten out the situation. She feels like she is constantly "putting out fires" and simply wants "structure and discipline so as to create a place for children to learn." Renna considers herself "the mother of the school." Again, the personal and professional are connected, essential to clear away the obstacles that preclude teaching and learning in her life and in her students' lives. Catherine wants "all her special education students to learn" and "is not sure she has ever or will ever walk away from a lesson thinking 'Today, everyone learned!'" as she thinks of herself "as only a teacher." Her daily obstacle "is never getting 100% success," a chronic thorn bush in her personal and professional life. After school and on weekends, Ashante runs Project Alpha, a program that supports young black men as they grapple with personal fears as they strive to achieve high goals and expectations. He struggles to "keep things real" because he is a "perfectionist with a profound fear of failure." He shares that he "will not attempt something if he thinks he will fail," a conflict that pervades every aspect of his life.

Each feels a personal responsibility not only to teach but also to provide a safe, supportive community that allows students to grapple with dilemmas of life and learning. Each works tirelessly to extirpate the thorn bush in the road in order to move on; for each, regressing or temporizing is not an option. When faced with difficult dilemmas, Darnell is frank and blatant: "Everybody is at least two people . . . we must adapt and be more than one person in order to deal with problems and differing viewpoints." Ashante agrees, commenting that a teacher must "first comfort and then teach," recounting how a young woman came to him that morning, "tears flowing down her face," requesting "one week's worth of work because her father committed suicide." Susan observes that "effective teaching requires compromising one's personal life, but that is fine, because it is exactly what I want to do." For these professionals, teaching is simultaneously lighting, walking through, and putting out fires.

KEEPING THE FIRES BURNING

To keep a lamp burning we have to keep putting oil in it.

—Mother Teresa

In February, as teachers read aloud and listen carefully to each other's personal missions, they not only identify common themes, patterns that pervade beliefs, but they also consider how mission statements reflect personal identity. One common theme is placing others first. Listeners comment that Susan "puts profession first, but that teaching is who she is so the personal and professional are intertwined." Susan also notes that occasionally, she "must observe" as she "cannot partake in everything, even though [she] wants to"; yet, observation is critical to effective teaching. Assaying the teaching context involves detailed observations. Observing is doing, and doing is teaching. Catherine also "puts teaching and students first and foremost." She "sees her [special needs] students as equals and ables." They are on a journey together and that journey defines her personally and professionally.

Renna simply "cares about those around her" and believes that "others feed off of what she feels, does, and experiences," which in turn keeps her fires burning. Josh "values relationships with others more than anything else," and these relationships help allay his "fear of failure," which results from a consistent and at times overwhelming sense of self-critique. His students make him feel valued, "keep him honest," and feed his fire. Darnell feels "blessed to exist, to be what it is that he is." He is "grateful, observant, and thankful for who he is and his life." Ashante observes that all "examine selves through their work and their students, contemplating where they are but more specifically what and who they are." Mariela is "heavily influenced by her past—family, teachers, and the bilingual program—and wants to inflect the benefits of her past onto her students." Each brings experience, honesty, altruism, passion, knowledge, and a continued sense of inquiry to classroom, students, and subjects. Consistent and continual commitment to keeping the fires burning pervades thought and action.

TEACHERS: ARSONISTS OF THE BEST KIND

It is not light that we need, but fire; it is not the gentle shower, but thunder. We need the storm, the whirlwind, and the earthquake.

—Frederick Douglass

Even April showers do not dampen the fires. Our teachers have written and probed written, spoken, and artistic mission statements, discussed moral and teaching philosophies, debated and reasoned through personal and professional dilemmas of life and practice, explained what they believe, why they believe, and how they believe. They have spoken, understood, and applied the word and the concept—epistemology—to their personal and professional lives. For these teachers personal and professional epistemologies are one and the same. Their words and actions suggest a genuine comfort with personal values that provide the principles that inform and guide their personal and professional decisions. The more experienced find intrinsic reward and happiness in their choices and are less concerned with external expectations, suggesting strongly constructed personal, foundational, and contextual knowledge (Baxter Magolda, 2002).

It is the end of our last meeting. Mariela, the most experienced of the group and a spitfire herself, comments: "There is so much energy and uniqueness in this room. If we do pass on who we are, can you imagine what the outcome could in fact be?" Ironically, they are unaware that they have been and continue to pass on who they are to others. Five years later, they are still teaching; passion for profession, subject, context, and students is *burned in*. They are not filling pails, but lighting fires. Like those whose rich art and genuine commitment are eloquently depicted throughout the poignant reflections in this text, they are teachers, arsonists of the best kind.

REFERENCES

Baxter Magolda, M. B. (2002). Epistemological reflection: The evolution of epistemological assumptions from age 18 to 30. In B. K. Hofer & P. R. Pintrich (Eds.), *Personal epistemology: The psychology of beliefs about knowledge and knowing* (pp. 89–102). Mahwah, NJ: Erlbaum.

Cohen, D. K., & Ball, D. L (1999). *Instruction, capacity, and improvement* (CPRE Research Report RR-43). Philadelphia: University of Pennsylvania, Consortium for Policy Research in Education, 1–35.

de Chardin, P. T. (2002). *Activation of energy: Enlightening reflections on spiritual energy.* New York: Harcourt.

Peige, J. (1977). *The essentials of fire fighting.* Stillwater: Oklahoma State University, Fire Protection Publications.

About the Editors
and Contributors

Audrey A. Friedman is an associate professor at the Lynch School of Education at Boston College (BC), where she teaches undergraduate and graduate methods courses in English and secondary education. Her research addresses the development of reflective judgment and cultural competence in preservice teachers. A former urban high school teacher, she still works with teachers and preservice teachers in schools. Audrey has received BC's Distinguished Faculty Teaching Award; the Mary Kaye Waldron Award, an honor awarded by undergraduates to faculty or an administrator "who has worked to enhance student life at Boston College"; and 2009 Professor of the Year for the State of Massachusetts, awarded by the Council for Advancement and Support of Education.

Luke Reynolds has taught 7th- through 12th-grade English in the public schools, as well as composition classes at Northern Arizona University, where he earned his M.A. in Creative Writing. He is coeditor with his wife, Jennifer, of the anthology *Dedicated to the People of Darfur: Writings on Fear, Risk, and Hope* (Rutgers University Press, 2009) and author of the nonfiction book *A New Man: Reclaiming Authentic Masculinity from a Culture of Pornography* (Stonegarden Publishing, 2007). Currently, Luke resides in York, England, with his wife and son. His Web site is http://www.lukewreynolds.com.

Jim Burke teaches English at Burlingame High School in California. He is the author of numerous books, including *What's the Big Idea? Question-Driven Units to Motivate Reading, Writing, and Thinking* (2010), *50 Essential Lessons: Tools and Techniques for Teaching English Language*

Arts (2007), *The English Teacher's Companion: A Complete Guide to Curriculum, Classroom, and the Profession* (2008), *Reading Reminders: Tools, Tips, and Techniques* (2001), and *Writing Reminders: Tools, Tips, and Techniques* (2003), all of which are published by Heinemann. He is also the author of *The Reader's Handbook* (2003, Great Source) and *Academic Workouts* (2006 First Choice Publishing). Jim is a senior consultant for the McDougal Littell Literature program. He has received numerous awards, including the NCTE Intellectual Freedom Award, the NCTE Conference on English Leadership Award, and the California Reading Association Hall of Fame Award. He served on the National Board for Professional Teaching Standards Committee on Adolescence and Young Adulthood English Language Arts Standards, as well as the College Board AP Exam and Course Review Commission.

Rosetta Marantz Cohen is Sylvia Dlugasch Bauman Professor of American Studies and Education at Smith College and also directs the college's internship program at the Smithsonian Museum. At Smith, she teaches courses on the history and philosophy of education and on nineteenth century American culture. She is the author of four books on school reform, teachers, and teaching, including *A Lifetime of Teaching: Portraits of Five Veteran High School Teachers* (1991, Teachers College Press), *The Work of Teachers in America: A Social History Through Stories* (1997, Erlbaum), and *The Teacher-Centered School* (2003, Scarecrow). Rosetta's best work on teachers has been done in collaboration with her husband, Samuel Scheer.

Christopher L. Doyle is a proud father, husband, teacher, and writer. He dedicates this essay to his students: past, present, and future.

Curt Dudley-Marling is a professor in the Lynch School of Education at Boston College. Before earning his doctorate at the University of Wisconsin–Madison he worked as an elementary special education teacher for 7 years in Ohio and Wisconsin. In the early 1990s he took a leave from his York University duties to teach third grade in Toronto, Canada. Curt has written extensively on issues of language and literacy, particularly the reading, writing, and language skills of struggling learners. He has also written numerous articles challenging the deficit thinking that dominates instruction for struggling learners, including students with disabilities. Overall, his work stands as a critique of deficit models that pathologize the language, culture, and experience of students from nondominant groups, their families, and their communities.

Michael Dunn is a new language arts supervisor who taught high school English for 17 years and served as a department leader. He spends the rest of his time with his wife, Kathleen, growing, and learning from, their four kids. Mike's favorite illusion is that his lifelong passion for the Red Sox has brought him closer to enlightenment, and his favorite motto is the quote Kathleen said on their first date, "Always make the extraordinary out of the ordinary." A graduate of Notre Dame, Mike earned his M.Ed. in educational administration from Teachers College, and has written several unpublished poems about teaching and parenting, as well as "Skateboarding the Third Rail: The Risk of the Middle" in Luke and Jennifer Reynolds's anthology *Dedicated to the People of Darfur: Writings on Risk, Hope, and Fear* (Rutgers University Press, 2009).

Peter Elbow is Professor Emeritus of English at the University of Massachusetts–Amherst. He directed the Writing Program there and at the State University of New York–Stony Brook, and taught at the Massachusetts Institute of Technology, Franconia College, and Evergreen State College. Peter has written numerous books and articles about writing and teaching writing. The Conference on English Education gave him the James Britton Award for *Everyone Can Write: Essays Toward a Hopeful Theory of Writing and Teaching Writing* (2000); NCTE gave him the James Squire Award for his transforming influence and lasting intellectual contribution; and in 2007 the Conference on College Composition and Communication (CCCC) gave him the Exemplar Award for representing the highest ideals of scholarship, teaching, and service. He is now finishing a book called *Vernacular Eloquence: Enlisting the Benefits of Speech for Writing.*

Andy Hargreaves holds the Brennan Chair in Education at the Lynch School of Education at Boston College. His research and activism encompass educational change, sustainable leadership, the emotions of teaching, teacher development and how to perform beyond expectations in education, business, and sport. His most recent books are the *Second International Handbook of Educational Change* (2010) with Michael Fullan, Ann Lieberman, and David Hopkins, and *The Fourth Way* (2009) with Dennis Shirley. Several of his books about teaching and change have received outstanding writing and book awards including *Change Wars* (2009) with Michael Fullan; *Teaching in the Knowledge Society* (2003); and *Changing Teachers; Changing Times* (1994).

Sam M. Intrator is a professor of education and child study and urban studies at Smith College in Northampton, MA. A former high school English teacher and administrator, his recent research and writing focus on understanding how youth experience out-of-school time and the relationship that out-of-school time programs have with formal school settings. He has written or edited five books, including *Tuned In and Fired Up: How Teaching Can Inspire Real Learning* (Yale University Press, 2003), which was a finalist for the prestigious Grawmeyer Award in Education. He also codirects Project Coach (PC), a youth leadership program that uses sports as a means to engage, connect, and develop a youth's capacity to serve others effectively. PC trains and employs teens as youth sport coaches for elementary-age children living in their communities.

James W. Loewen's gripping retelling of American history as it should— and could—be taught, *Lies My Teacher Told Me* (1995, New Press), has sold more than 1,000,000 copies and continues to inspire K–16 teachers to get students to challenge, rather than memorize, their textbooks. James taught race relations for 20 years at the University of Vermont. Previously he taught at Tougaloo College in Mississippi. He has also written *Lies Across America: What Our Historic Sites Get Wrong* (2007, Simon & Schuster). Most recently, Teachers College Press published *Teaching What Really Happened* (2010), intended to give K–12 teachers (and prospective teachers) solutions to the problems pointed out in Loewen's earlier works. He has been an expert witness in more than 50 civil rights, voting rights, and employment cases. Currently, he lives in Washington, D.C., continuing his research on how Americans remember their past, and is also Distinguished Lecturer for the Organization of American Historians.

Gregory Michie has spent the past 20 years working as a teacher and teacher educator in Chicago. He is the author of *Holler If You Hear Me: The Education of a Teacher and His Students* (2009, Teachers College Press), an account of his experiences teaching in Chicago Public Schools, and co-editor of *City Kids, City Schools: More Reports from the Front Row* (2008, New Press). Currently, he teaches in the Department of Foundations, Social Policy, and Research at Concordia University in Chicago.

Linda Nathan is the founding headmaster of the Boston Arts Academy, the city's first and only public high school for the visual and performing arts. Under her leadership, the school has won state, national, and international recognition and awards. Linda was also a driving force behind the creation of Fenway High School. She is a cofounder and board member of the Center for Collaborative Education, a nonprofit education reform organization. Fluent in Spanish, Linda has worked on issues of school reform in Puerto Rico, Argentina, and Colombia, as well as Brazil. She has written a book about teaching and leadership in urban schools, *The Hardest Questions Aren't on the Test*, which was recently translated into Spanish. Linda earned a bachelor's degree at the University of California–Berkeley, a master's degree in education administration at Antioch University, a master of performing arts degree at Emerson College, and a doctorate in education at Harvard University.

Sonia Nieto, who has taught students from elementary school through doctoral studies, is Professor Emerita of Education at the University of Massachusetts–Amherst. Her research focuses on multicultural education, teacher education, and the education of Latinos, immigrants, and other students of culturally and linguistically diverse backgrounds. Her books include *Affirming Diversity: The Sociopolitical Context of Multicultural Education* (5th ed., 2008, with Patty Bode); *The Light in Their Eyes: Creating Multicultural Learning Communities* (10th anniversary edition, 2010); and *What Keeps Teachers Going?* (2003); along with three edited volumes: *Puerto Rican Students in U.S. Schools* (2000); *Why We Teach* (2005); and *Dear Paulo: Letters from Those Who Dare Teach* (2008). She serves on several regional and national advisory boards that focus on educational equity and social justice, and she has received many academic and community awards for her scholarship, advocacy, and activism, including four honorary doctorates.

Kirsten Olson is an educational activist, writer, teacher, and professional developer. She works with public, private, and alternative schools all over the country on issues of school culture, leadership development, and creating more engaging learning environments for everyone in school. She is the author of *Wounded by School: Recapturing the Joy in Learning and Standing Up to Old School Culture,* which was one of the bestselling books at Teachers College Press last year, and *Schools as Colonizers* (2008, VDM Verlag), about the radical school writers of the 1960s. She has been a consultant to the Bill and Melinda Gates Foundation, the Kennedy School at Harvard University, and the Massachusetts Center for Charter Public School Excellence. She received a doctorate from the Harvard Graduate School of Education, and was an English major at Vassar College. Kirsten's group blog on educational transformation, Cooperative Catalyst, is a place where teachers and administrators are gathering to talk about educational change. Join us there!

Parker Palmer is founder and senior partner of the Center for Courage & Renewal (http://www.CourageRenewal.org). Author of eight books—including *A Hidden Wholeness* (2009), *Let Your Life Speak* (2000), and *The Courage to Teach* (1997)—he holds a Ph.D. in sociology from the University of California at Berkeley and 10 honorary doctorates. In 1998 the Leadership Project, a national survey of 10,000 educators, named him one of the 30 "most influential senior leaders" in higher education and one of the 10 key "agenda-setters" of the past decade. In 2005 Jossey-Bass published *Living the Questions: Essays Inspired by the Work and Life of Parker J. Palmer* in his honor.

Sam Scheer is a high school teacher in Windsor, Connecticut, and the author (with wife Rosetta Cohen) of two books on education and teaching, *The Work of Teachers in America: A Social History Through Stories* (1997) and *Teacher–Centered Schools: Reimagining Educational Reform in the 21st Century* (2003). He is currently involved in Project Opening Doors, a program funded by the Gates Foundation and the Exxon Corporation, to expand minority enrollment in Advanced Placement courses. Scheer sits on the editorial board of the *Journal of Modern Literature* (JML). He holds a B.A. from Bennington College and an M.Phil. from Oxford University.

Patricia A. Wasley is currently a professor of Educational Leadership and Policy Studies at the University of Washington, College of Education. She served as Dean of the College from 2000 through August 2010 and was the Dean of the Bank Street College of Education from 1996 through August 2000. From 1989 through 1996, Patricia served as a Senior Researcher for School Change at the Coalition of Essential Schools at Brown University. Before that she served as a high school teacher and administrator in the public schools. Her current work revolves around rethinking colleges of education and American high schools. She has written several books and a number of articles about teaching, teachers, and high school reform.

Zoe Weil is the cofounder and president of the Institute for Humane Education (http://www.HumaneEducation.org). She created the first Master of Education and Certificate programs in Humane Education in the United States. She is the author of several books, including Nautilus Silver Medal winner *Most Good, Least Harm: A Simple Principle for a Better World and Meaningful Life* (2009); *The Power and Promise of Humane Education* (2004); *Above All, Be Kind: Raising a Humane Child in Challenging Times* (2003), and Moonbean Gold Medal winner for juvenile fiction, *Claude and Medea* (2007). Zoe leads workshops and speaks widely across the United States and Canada about humane education and humane living. She blogs at http://www.zoeweil.com.

Index